Our Divine Destiny

A Saul Book

D1613223

Dictated to John Smallman

For further information contact John Smallman at:
saulthebook@gmail.com

ISBN 978-0-557-53205-6

1 Humanity is ready to move into the brilliant light of fully-conscious living

The prayers and hopes and desires that humans hold deep in their hearts are rapidly coming into alignment and agreement. The majority of you want peace, tranquility, joy, harmony, and abundance for yourselves and for all others. The inadequacy of your old methods of solving problems and trying to live together in reasonable peace and cooperation has been most unsatisfactory and disappointing.

Finally all are beginning to realize this, and are beginning to release their anger and fear which have made harmonious existence impossible before now. This realization began to dawn just after the end of the World War II, as people started getting

1

their lives back together and saw the incredible destruction the war had caused all over the planet, and the vast number who had become destitute, refugees, or both. And despite the war being over — a war that was supposed to have brought peace to the world — a great divide between East and West had formed which threatened to cause even greater wars.

People were tired. War had exhausted them, and yet the outlook appeared to be more war. So, for many, this was a great awakening, a realization that there must be a better way. This desire, this hope for a new way of living began to grow, fueled by the noise of political disagreement and ferocious argument. Other wars confirmed what people knew in their hearts: war solves nothing; it only aggravates and intensifies the fear and distrust that it causes in the first place.

So the desire for peace and harmony spread and became an ever-strengthening prayer to God for divine intervention — not to win a war, but to cease all war. And this was the cry — the call for help, true help, to save humanity and the planet — that God wanted to hear. It was the sign, the indication that humanity was growing up and could put to most positive use the divine energy that has always been available.

And so, from the mid-twentieth century onwards, massive quantities have been pouring down on Planet Earth, bringing great waves of healing, compassion, forgiveness, acceptance, and love, which humans have been directing towards each other with increasing hope and enthusiasm. Some of the results are very visible — such as the removal of the death penalty in many places on the planet, the great movement to establish human rights for all, and the increasing acceptance of different lifestyles.

The effects of this outpouring of divine Love to Planet Earth for even such a short period of time have been quite stupendous.

And now, as a result, the whole planet is bathed in divine energy that is being absorbed and passed on, and more and more people are feeling the effects. This is why humanity is now ready to move from its narrow and blinkered perception of life and what it means to be human into the brilliant, divine Light of fully-conscious living, where God's Presence everywhere in His divine creation is fully apparent and most wonderful to behold and experience.

You have shut yourselves off from God's Presence and from the limitless possibilities for joy for far to long. Now you are about to come home. Your joy and happiness will be boundless, as all very shortly falls into place, and you awaken into the bliss and the celebrations that your return Home will generate. The moment of awakening is very, very close.

ϴ   ϴ   ϴ

2   Change of an amazing kind is in the air

As the moment for humanity to return to a state of full consciousness approaches, it will become very apparent to all that change of a most amazing kind is in the air.

Very, very many humans know, deep within themselves, that a great change in the way they live and perceive life is essential if humanity is to survive on Planet Earth. They also feel that something of great importance is about to occur . . . and of course it is. This feeling — this sense that an event of unimaginable magnitude is pending — is indeed the first sign of a planetwide awakening.

Allowing this feeling to grow and strengthen leads to an opening of the awareness to information that has long been available, but has remained unperceived. This opening of awareness that

3

so many are now beginning to experience is uplifting and inspiring for them. It brings a sense of personal validation and optimism to their lives, even though the problems and difficulties they are experiencing may have become more intense: long-buried emotions of a negative nature are coming to the surface and must be acknowledged, addressed, and released.

Many are truly realizing that in order for peace, happiness, and contentment to fill their lives they must forgive. This also means forgiving themselves for their own inadequacies and for their less-than-generous treatment of others.

Previously, this treatment of others had appeared to them to be normal and reasonable in the dangerous world in which they were living. Now, realization is bursting in on their awareness that the world is dangerous mainly because of their own unreasonable behavior. This is at first a quite shocking and unsettling discovery. But as God's Love inundates your planet and begins to seep into the hearts of even the most hurt and damaged among you, a deep knowing wells up, showing you and assuring you that to act from your heart center with unconditional love, acceptance, and forgiveness will indeed change the world.

The awareness that your attitudes and perceptions must change if you are to survive is accompanied by a sense that it is definitely going to happen . . . is in fact happening as you think about it. It is from this sense — this deep inner knowing — that your optimism is arising, and you know that it is totally justified!

And yet, of course, you still have doubts. They are strongly ingrained after so many eons of disharmony, confusion, pain, and fear. However, you *can* feel them dissolving. Allow that to happen — do not hold onto them — you no longer need them.

Relax. Put yourselves regularly and frequently into that inner place of peace that each one of you possesses . . . and let go. Your peace, your knowledge of your divine connection and of your complete acceptability will increase and intensify enormously. As it does so, you will absolutely know that the same thing is happening to millions of others as you move toward that wonderful moment when you burst forth into the state of full consciousness from which you have truly never departed, and which it is the Creator's Will that you shall dwell in permanently.

It is almost upon you! Allow yourselves to know it, believe in it, and enjoy with eager anticipation the short period remaining before it occurs.

⊖   ⊖   ⊖

3   Many of you feel that something of great moment is about to occur

Your world, Planet Earth — a truly divine planet in the sense that it is presently being absolutely inundated with our Creator's abundant, unconditional Love — is ready for change, and is demanding change.

She has suffered enormously in recent years at the hands of man, and she has had enough. She knows that you are supposed to be her guardians, that you have been seriously confused and misled, and that you have basically — quite unwittingly — fallen down on the job. Now that has to change.

Humanity is being prepared for this great change. Many of you sense it. You are not at all sure what it is that you are sensing and expecting, but you feel sure that something of great moment is about to occur. And your senses, your intuitions are not misleading you. They are assisting you to prepare, so that when this momentous series of events starts to occur, you will not go into terminal shock, but will open yourselves to become unobstructed conduits through which God's unconditional Love can flow with a force and vitality never before experienced on Planet Earth.

The preparations have — in your human sense of time — been going on for eons. And now, as they are completed, the divine energies of abundant, unconditional Love will flow into you and through you to bring you to your rightful state of full consciousness. There is very little that you actually have to do to assist in bringing this state into being.

You all knowingly incarnated to be on Earth at this time because your presence was essential to bring this particular stage of God's magnificent, ongoing, creative endeavor to completion. You are holding the intent that all will come to fruition as divinely planned and intended — and so it shall. Just desiring it, hoping for it, and longing for it is what you came to do, and you are truly doing that — even if you are unaware of it.

The number of different ways in which you are holding and anchoring the Light and Intent is quite astounding. None of you are here by chance or accident; you each have a role to play and you are playing it magnificently.

As you sense and feel the energies for change all around you, tune into them, accept them, and intend to be a conduit through which they can flow unrestricted, to usher in the magnificent new Golden Age that will bring peace, joy, and harmony to all on Earth.

In an instant, suffering, pain, despair, disillusionment, and disharmony will just evaporate like morning mist that the sun burns off, and you will all find yourselves in a state of joy and peace that at present you are unable to imagine or understand.

The Creator's divine Power is mind-blowing, magnificent in

the extreme, and you are all about to share It as you help to bring in the New Age for which you have been longing.

Just continue to want it, and in your prayers, your meditations, your periods of quiet relaxation, believe that it is about to happen. Enjoy with eager anticipation this last short period of time before all becomes clear to you, as you burst forth into the infinite joy and bliss that is the state of full consciousness.

The Kingdom of Heaven awaits you. So be ready to be there . . . and you will — in an instant — because in truth you are already there. You just have not learned to experience it.

ⴲ   ⴲ   ⴲ

4   Major changes are being planned and implemented

As this stage of God's plan for humanity approaches completion, much is occurring on levels to which you do not have access at present that will amaze and delight you.

For a very long time (as you experience it) life as a human has been fraught with difficulty, pain, and disappointment. But that is all about to change. Over the last few decades, awareness of your true nature, your spiritual heritage, has been growing rapidly. Nearly all of humanity is aware that major changes in the way you all live and interact on Planet Earth are essential to your well-being.

Awareness of need makes change possible. And that awareness of need is allowing and encouraging the necessary changes to be planned and implemented. A far more loving and compassionate way of dealing with the organization and problem-solving aspects of the many human societies and cultures presently inhabiting Earth will shortly come into effect. It is the result of much careful thought and planning in the realms that are currently hidden from you, and which will become visible as a great wave of Love and understanding sweeps across the planet. In its wake will come major changes in every field of human endeavor. Confrontation and violent disagreement will decrease in intensity and as harmonious cooperation becomes widespread will cease altogether.

A true Golden Age of harmony, peace, and abundance is dawning for Planet Earth and all her inhabitants.

There will indeed be much joy as the new systems that humanity will adopt — to help them solve the planet's outstanding problems of scarcity and pollution — come into operation. Many of you have already been trained in the operation and maintenance of these new systems so that they may replace the old and inappropriate ones with a minimum of disorder and confusion.

The age of fear and anxiety is coming to an end. The new systems of organization, manufacturing, and distribution are, by your present standards, incredibly clean, efficient, and economical. All your needs will be provided for abundantly without creating vast quantities of waste and pollution. And the polluting waste that you have been creating in ever greater quantities will be safely and efficiently recycled, to aid in returning Earth to her original state of perfection and beauty.

This time in Earth's history is a great one indeed, as eons of strife and suffering are rapidly replaced by an environment in which peace, harmony, cooperation, and abundance make life a joy for all humanity.

Disease, dysfunction, anger, and fear will dissolve as all realize that there is absolutely no need to continue creating these divisive and unhappy conditions. Prepare to enjoy your wonderful release from bondage and subjugation as you return to the freedom that has always been your rightful heritage.

Θ   Θ   Θ

5   The apparent chaos is not purposeless

The apparent chaos across the world is not purposeless. Despite the pain, anger, poverty, and manipulation at the human level, much is being cleared at deep spiritual levels in preparation for humanity's new enlightened existence on your perfectly healed and renewed Planet Earth.

The profound transformations in attitude and perception required for living in this new Golden Age of peace and abundance are occurring at a rapidly increasing rate across the planet, as more of you respond to the spiritual reawakening that is unfolding within all of you. You are becoming very aware of this need for change, and you are making these changes with renewed enthusiasm because you are discovering that you feel better and more alive with each spiritually guided change that you make. *Acceptance-of-what-is* has incredible power to dissolve even the most stubbornly ingrained habits and blockages that discourage introspection and the resultant awareness that leads to healthy change.

Your earthly environment is now in the process of cleansing and healing itself after millennia of abuse, and this is leading to a greatly expanded awareness of the damage that has been done to the planet, and an intense desire to re-establish sane and loving practices that will nurture and enhance the planet for the delight of all.

6 You are not lost, forgotten waifs!

There continue to be many things happening in the Earth plane that are divinely guided and intended and that remain hidden from the vast majority of humans.

God's plan for His human sons and daughters is quite magnificent, and very soon you will start to become aware of it. The lives you are presently dreaming are set to become far happier and saner as the Holy Spirit nudges you towards an experiential awareness of who you truly are — perfect reflections of your divine Father, who loves you utterly and completely without reservation. You are perfect just the way He created you, and that is how He sees you all.

You are all going to become aware of that much sooner than you think, because the intense love that a very small percentage of you have been practicing is having undreamt-of repercussions throughout your human environment.

You are not lost, forgotten waifs! You are perfect offspring of the Supreme Being—God— in all His magnificence and glory. And so you, too, are glorious.

You are very soon to awaken, know, and experience that most wonderful uplifting Reality of unimaginable joy that is your divine heritage. Truly do not believe your dreams of scarcity, pain, and despair. Know that you are only dreaming this unhappy state in which you experience loss, separation, and abandonment, and that you are about to awaken into the most fantastic and beautiful Light of God's eternal Presence, in which you are eternally present in every moment of your existence. Nothing else is possible!

You are alive and well in every moment, and yet you know it not. But your unpleasant and disturbing dream is approaching its point of termination. It will be no more as you awaken into the wonder and joy of living eternally in the divine Presence where you are in every moment of your existence.

How could it be otherwise? Because there is only God. So where He is is where you are, always, and forever. There is no other possibility. The only existence there is, is in God's divine Presence in every moment, without break or interruption of any kind.

You are always at Home in His Presence, and you are about to awaken into that Reality — the only possible Reality that *is* All That Exists.

ϴ   ϴ   ϴ

7   This is what full-conscious awareness is all about

When you move into full consciousness, you will no longer find yourselves wondering what life is all about. You will *know* what it is all about, as your inner knowing wells up from the (presently hidden and therefore mostly unrecognized) deepest center of your being.

You will be filled with an all-encompassing and incredibly powerful sense of self-worth, validity, and purposeful direction. You will know why you exist and what your purpose is in every moment. And this knowing will fill you with contentment, satisfaction, and the abundant energy you need to fulfill your creative desires perfectly.

This is what full-conscious awareness is all about: the absolute certainty — with the divine wisdom and knowledge necessary to know this — that you are doing in every moment exactly what you want and intend, and that it is totally and perfectly in agreement with the divine Will and Intent.

It is impossible to describe for you in any meaningful way the joy, the bliss, and the exhilaration that you will experience, as you live — once again — fully in the Presence of, and united with, the divine Creator.

Θ   Θ   Θ

8   No one — absolutely no one — is excluded

The divine plan is truly awesome, and the joy, satisfaction, and happiness that it will bring to humanity is indeed beyond words. Its astonishingly detailed nature, which provides unique personal experiences for all on Earth, is mind-boggling.

Each one of you on Earth will experience — individually — directed entirely to you — the unconditional Love of the Creator. Despite the vastness of His creation He will direct to each one of you His infinite Love and affection. His power and ability to single out and individuate — so that all feel personally loved and recognized while at the same instant drawing all together to experience the Oneness — is truly awesome.

Your delight, as He has always promised, will be total and complete. You will want for nothing, because everything you desire will be provided instantly. All you have to do is to accept, and once you know Him — truly *know* Him with every particle of your self-hood and beingness — you will accept Him and His divine gifts completely and unconditionally.

The experience of unification with the One, the divine Being, is utterly and completely magnificent in every way. Your joy, His joy, the joy of all creation as this stage in the divine plan comes swiftly to completion is absolutely and completely beyond description.

All are included in the divine plan. No one — absolutely no

one — is excluded, because unconditional divine Love is all-inclusive, utterly accepting, and non-judgmental. And as all are the One, all will accept all, unconditionally, as does the Creator. That is why all relationship problems, whether on an intimate one-to-one or a nation-to-nation basis, will simply evaporate, as love, wisdom, understanding, respect, and compassion flow in to suffuse every individual on the planet.

Yes, there will be a few — a very, very small percentage of Earth's population — who will reject what is being offered, but their influence, their ability to disrupt this magnificent coming-together of all races, nations, tribes, and religious, political, and social groups into one wondrous family will be negligible.

The new environment that they will choose to inhabit will provide everything they could possibly require to lead them, when they are ready, back to the divine realm that, as with all of humanity, is their destination and their Home.

All will return Home, none will be lost, because the Creator's patience, compassion, and unconditional love for all of His creation is total — totally inclusive, and totally accepting. The magnificence that He has planned for His creation will be experienced by His creation just as He has always intended. Not even *one* will be excluded because He *is* Love — and Love is totally inclusive.

ϴ   ϴ   ϴ

9   Many wonderful people are preparing to bring in great changes

As humanity's spiritual awareness grows stronger in every moment, big changes in the way you live your lives and treat each other will occur. The anger, fear, pain, and disharmony that prevails in many areas will ease, as the next generation of leaders, armed with a greater understanding of human psychology moves into your governmental systems. They will prove far more flexible and much wiser than their predecessors, and will have a true respect for the rights and dignity of the individual. They will work for peace and harmony for all and will have no hidden personal agendas causing conflicts of interest and leading to the deceit and corruption that appear to be endemic within human society.

Great changes are on the way and many wonderful people are preparing to bring them in with enormous assistance from the spiritual realms.

The peace and harmony, for which so many of you have been praying for so long, are truly starting to permeate societies throughout the planet with increasing effectiveness. In your lifetime, the way in which humans view each other is going to change far more radically and dramatically than the incredible technological changes that you have witnessed during the last two decades. As the old saying goes: "You ain't seen nothin' yet!"

Keep up your schedule of regular prayer and meditation, as this provides a most powerful flow of love that influences in many wonderful ways the planet and all who dwell there. Your prayers and meditations, your intents and desires for change are most effective and operate cumulatively, building a huge wave that inundates all in its path with the energy of Love. It is an energy so powerful that there truly is no meaningful way to describe it — it can only be experienced. And when you experience it, it leaves absolutely no doubts as to what it is.

So, as I said, continue to meditate, and know that you will be swept up into permanent, indescribable bliss as you return to full consciousness and full awareness of your unbreakable connection to your divine Father.

It is your birthright — you will claim it! And your joy will know no bounds.

Ө   Ө   Ө

10   As humanity moves forward expectantly

As humanity moves forward expectantly and enthusiastically toward full consciousness, it will become apparent to all that their spiritual yearnings will soon be achieved.

All are sensing the new intense energies of divine Love that are enveloping your beautiful planet, and are starting to feel powerfully guided to seek the true meaning of their lives as humans. It is a rich but somewhat unsettling experience as they awaken to the awareness that their lives have a much deeper meaning and purpose than they had ever considered possible.

Until very recently, most humans found life to be a very limiting experience, dictated by the circumstances and location of their physical births. A small minority had visibly moved beyond those general limitations to positions of apparent prestige, power, fame, or notoriety, and were envied or admired. Yet they too seemed to suffer from most of the problems experienced by everyone else; they just had more wealth and more advisers to help them deal with these challenges. So even though their lives might appear more glamorous or seductive, they themselves were obviously no happier.

Now that the knowledge of the damage that humanity has inflicted on Planet Earth — by its thoughtless, greedy, arrogant, and in fact, insane behavior — has become firmly established in everyone's awareness, it is clear to all that this way of living must cease. People are seeking alternatives that will provide a sustainable environment for their children, and for their children's children. They are beginning to perceive a bigger picture — a picture that is no longer limited to the mundane everyday process of feeding and sheltering their families and being able to pay their bills.

A larger vision *is* needed, and growing numbers of you are becoming aware of this, and aware that the way you live and behave does most definitely affect others. It is apparent now that what you do as an individual has far wider repercussions than was previously realized.

Of course this first became apparent as the affect that others' thoughtless behavior had on you. For a long time humanity has been struggling with the problem of how to fix or correct the thoughtlessness or misguided actions of others. Now, finally, it is becoming ever more apparent that you can only fix your own behavior, and moreover, that when you do, almost miraculously, others start to fix theirs.

It leads to the realization that you are all connected, that there is a divine Being — a divine Intelligence whose nature is benign and loving. And so, more and more of you are praying, meditating, and seeking to connect with this Being, and in so doing finding peace and a considerable easing of life's stresses and anxieties.

Humanity is finally becoming aware of and starting to accept that it has a divine heritage that will provide everything it needs for its survival — abundantly, and with joy.

The search for that experience is intensifying as are the divine energies pouring into each one of you.

Full consciousness is your divine state of being in which all is clear to you, and your life experience is one of absolute joy and unconditional love. And that is the state toward which you are all moving with increasing speed.

Soon you will be in total rapture!

ϴ   ϴ   ϴ

11   The choice to incarnate as a human is indeed very courageous

As a human progresses through life, many wonderful opportunities are presented to him so that he may make the most of his human existence. Frequently, however, these opportunities are not seen or recognized but seem only to be situations that have developed inexplicably, without any obvious cause, and which now have to be rectified as they interfere with or inhibit the person's worldly plans.

It is as though you went shopping and bought some items that you knew would be of use and value to you. However, on arriving home, you forgot that you had bought anything and discarded the items complete with their packaging into the trash bin. Later, when you find yourself in need of them, you go out and purchase them again, still not remembering that you had already bought them for use in this eventuality and had thrown them away.

This inability as a human to remember the details of the life

18

path you created before you incarnated does tend to make life quite confusing for you. If you simply accept life's occurrences as random events over which you have no control, it becomes very difficult for you to reconnect consciously with the fact that your life most definitely has a meaning and purpose, which you with great wisdom gave it so that it could teach you and guide you to new levels of spiritual awareness.

Many incarnations occur to enable an entity to re-experience lessons from previous incarnations which had passed by unnoticed and unlearned!

To take human form and incarnate on Earth in order to learn and grow from your preplanned life path is a very onerous and demanding task. However, when you complete the course and free yourself from the need to reincarnate, the rewards you receive for having chosen the human experience are indeed absolutely magnificent.

Life, knowledge, consciousness, awareness, experience, wisdom and love come from deep within an entity, and there are many ways that she can choose to travel on that inward journey of self-discovery that leads her back to Oneness with her Creator.

The choice to make that journey as a human is indeed very courageous because it is such a demanding path to follow, with its frequently experienced sense of confusion, inadequacy, abandonment, and utter desolation. But of course the upside is the tremendous sense of wonder and achievement when the journey is completed, and the entity once more enters into the Light, to be engulfed and enraptured by the experience of being once more overwhelmed by the Love of God.

Words can never even attempt to describe the sensation that the entity experiences when this journey is completed, because there are an infinite number of ways in which this divine bliss can be experienced, and each entity chooses her own unique way to do so, thus adding to the infinite creative wonder that is All That Is. When the entity completes her journey, the state of infinite bliss that she then achieves adds enormously to the bliss of all the others who have already arrived home.

There is no end to the bliss that can and will be experienced — satiation, saturation or drowning are not possible in a state of divine bliss! Just know that when you complete your self-appointed and self-chosen task the rewards will be infinitely beyond your wildest dreams.

So never give up! Keep pushing forward. It is quite impossible for you to fail. Your loving Father could never permit entities to set themselves tasks that were beyond their abilities to complete with total success. You are all winners of an infinitely grand prize. Complete the journey; come home, and claim your inheritance!

Ɵ   Ɵ   Ɵ

12   There is a most wonderful purpose

Humanity's spiritual evolution continues to progress rapidly, and those who favor forceful control and manipulation of others are increasingly in a minority.

The divine plan and intent for humans is that they shall move into their rightful state of full consciousness. When that happens, as it will very soon, all knowledge, all information will be instantly available — truly, it already is; you just have not yet learned to access it — and the meaning of existence, of creation will be absolutely clear.

There is indeed a most wonderful purpose to All That Is and to the ongoing creative endeavor that that establishes and maintains. As you all become aware of this, you will find yourselves filled with the most uplifting and delightful sense of peace and tranquility, as you finally understand what creation, God, All That Is really means.

Everything that you perceive will be totally beautiful and wondrous. As your awareness opens to this realization your joy will be boundless, and the essential nature of your own place in the divine creation will be abundantly clear.

Eons of time — as you experience it on Earth — have passed while this divine plan has taken shape and progressed towards this stage of completion. And yet in spiritual terms it has always been complete, with the outcome precisely defined and demonstrated since the moment it was spontaneously created in the mind of God. Everything — as humanity is starting to realize — has always been and always will be. It is only humanity's perception and ability to understand that appears to change.

The state of full consciousness that you are soon to experience is changeless, yet always progressing and developing. In your present state of limited perception and awareness this is a paradox that is quite incomprehensible, and yet the fact that you cannot understand it, despite all your unsuccessful efforts to do so, does in some strange way give you satisfaction and hope. It appears to confirm for you that there is a benign, unconditionally loving Intelligence running the show.

You know deep within yourselves that you are not alone, that you never have been, and that all is always perfectly well in the divine Kingdom. And this knowingness shows up quite frequently in your creative arts — dance, drama, music, poetry, and painting — which is why people are so drawn to them. Whenever humans create something of beauty in any field of endeavor, it brings joy and hope to countless others and helps them to continue their movement forward on the path of spiritual growth.

And your rate of progress has indeed increased enormously, as divinely intended, during the last few decades of your earthly existence. You are rapidly approaching the moment when this stage of the divine plan will be completed, bringing untold joy to you all and, of course, to all of creation.

Your divine destiny of infinite joy and happiness is almost upon you. Hang in there as it comes to fruition.

Ө   Ө   Ө

13 Your world leaders are in the grip of a personal crisis

Much has indeed been happening. Your world leaders find themselves in rather a quandary as their popular support dwindles, both among the general population and in their councils and cabinets.

Many people are feeling betrayed as it becomes apparent how badly they have misled you. Trust in the political process is waning rapidly, and the desire for change and for political and governmental integrity and honesty is creating a groundswell of discontent that is leading towards great change and upheaval in your social structures.

A majority of the world's population, for the first time in recorded history, believe that war and violence are no longer options for solving disagreements of any kind, and that feeling is found in all levels of society. Those who make their living in combative spheres of activity are becoming severely disillusioned, and those who would lead and control them are losing the ability to do so.

Your leaders are being inundated with unconditional love and, as it sweeps over them and immerses them, they find themselves in the grip of personal crises as they begin to see their very selfish agendas in a new light. This change in perception is most alarming for them. They are well aware that it is a perception shared by millions, but it is one they have dismissed as impractical and weak-minded as they jockeyed very competitively for positions of power and influence on the world stage. Now their doubts about the agendas they have been pursuing so forcefully and enthusiastically are erupting into their awareness, and they find themselves no longer able to suppress or dismiss them as had been their customary way of dealing with them.

It is a shocking experience — one that they had never before come up against — and it is leaving them dazed and perplexed. There is no one with whom any of them can acknowledge it, let alone safely discuss it, and this causes substantial anxiety. Some are close to panic, which is not an emotion to which they are accustomed. It does not sit well with their normal mode of operation, namely, to divide, manipulate, and control. It is an emotion they are accustomed to seeing and provoking in others, and to find it threatening to overcome them is distracting, disorienting, and indeed scary.

As you have been informed by many sources of the Light, major changes are about to occur at every level of human society. They have been divinely planned and orchestrated for eons of Earth time, and are now about to bear fruit.

The results of these changes will be quite awesome, as people from all walks of life and every area of the world unite in a spirit of loving and harmonious cooperation to bring peace, healing, acceptance, forgiveness, and abundance to all on Planet Earth. The speed and efficacy with which these changes take effect will amaze and delight you all, and the realization that a peaceful, joyful, and harmonious existence for all on the planet is not only possible but is occurring, will be the final completion of a dream that you have been hoping for, desiring, and intending for so long.

Celebration and joy are in the air, and as it comes into being, all sense or expression of fear, anxiety, anger, helplessness, and oppression will dissolve. Even your panic-stricken leaders will be filled with a sense of relief and happiness as it becomes apparent to them that their defenses — psychological and physical — are completely unnecessary, and that they too can enter into the celebrations with total freedom from inhibitions or concerns of any kind.

Gaiety and laughter will sweep through your lives. The arrival of this most awesome moment is almost upon you. Just hold the Light and hold the intent!

Θ Θ Θ

14   Life on Earth is no accident

Life on Earth as a human is no accident. It is definitely not as a result of random, favorable environmental conditions that life was created on Planet Earth. Favorable environmental conditions were created on the planet so that humanity would be able to grow and develop there, because humanity is needed on the planet.

The divine plan for humanity is awe-inspiring and utterly wonderful, and humans on Earth are just now beginning to achieve the level of spiritual development necessary to fulfill the Creator's Intent and take their place in the vast spiritual organization that is developing in this area of the universe.

As each individual human continues to develop her spirituality with ever-increasing rapidity, she will become more aware of a strong inner knowing that she, like every other human, is absolutely irreplaceable in the divine creative endeavor. There are no failures; every human being is, and will always continue to be, a resounding success. This will become joyfully obvious to each of you as your spiritual development raises your level of awareness, allowing your consciousness to mingle more and more with the divine Consciousness, giving you ever-deeper insights into what the Creator, in His infinite Love and Wisdom, has planned and intends.

The meaning of Love will become more visibly apparent to you as you experience its energy and power in every area of your existence. You will find yourselves able only to love, and only desiring and intending to love. Any anger, resentment, judgment, hate, irritation, or dissatisfaction with others will dissolve and slip out of your lives as you begin to recognize the spark of divinity that shines brilliantly in every human — without exception.

Where a human has acted out of negative emotions or beliefs in a self-centered way, you will see that the individual has suffered damage and is recovering, and you will flood him with love, compassion, and healing to speed him along on his magnificent spiritual path. You will all become great lovers of humanity when you begin to see and comprehend the wonders that God has instilled in each and every human. Your compassion will know no bounds, and an epidemic of love will spread with the speed of a gale-blown forest fire, infecting all with God's infinite Love, which He continuously pours forth abundantly on His beloved creation.

Every single one of you is infinitely loved, and that will become overwhelmingly apparent to you, and you will find yourselves linked most wonderfully into the love chain that connects humanity to God — All That Is.

For each of you there is a place that suits you absolutely perfectly, in which you will find yourself totally accepted and divinely happy. What more could you possibly ask for?

God loves you — infinitely. He has prepared a place for you — and you will come Home to it.

Know that . . . . Believe that . . . . And relax into the certainty that that is where you are headed, and that that is where you will arrive — in fact, truly you are there already; it is just that your awareness, your consciousness has not yet awakened to this most wonderful Reality. However, very soon it will, and your amazement and exhilaration as you return Home will be most wonderful for you to experience; and for us awaiting you here, most wonderful to behold!

Ө Ө Ө

15   The suddenness of its arrival will astound all

As you wait with great hope and expectancy during this lull before the arrival of the new Golden Age for which you have all been working and praying for so long, just relax and allow the divine energy to pour into you during your meditations. This will strengthen and inspire you in preparation for the big event.

It truly is an event of breath-taking importance, because it will totally change the way you experience life and existence — permanently. The joy and happiness that will flood into your lives will be overwhelming. The suddenness of its arrival will astound all. And the shock will be great and wonderful, like a child on his birthday, when he awakens to find that the gift that

26

he most wanted and yet dared not hope for was waiting by his bed.

It is impossible to describe to you, let alone prepare you for the joy and wonder that all of humanity is about to experience. Life truly is about to become the most blissful experience imaginable for all of you, wherever you live on the planet. All barriers to hope, trust, joy, and love are about to fall, and a great inrush of understanding, acceptance, forgiveness, and healing is about to engulf you, enabling all to see and experience the fact that we truly are all One, and that the joy of One is the joy of All.

The Creator's divine plan for His creation is wonderful beyond comprehension, and all are about to be enfolded into the divine conscious awareness that provides for every possible and imaginable desire — instantly.

So continue to pray and meditate, because this will intensify the ability of the divine energies of peace to flow in and suffuse your whole being in preparation for this swiftly approaching, momentous, divine event. As I have told you before, it has been planned since the beginning of human existence, and its time is upon you. Your divine Creator wants and intends that you experience — permanently — love, joy, and abundance; and because that is His divine Intent, and because it is also your heart's desire, then so you shall. Relax and prepare yourselves to receive this gift for which you have been longing.

Any remaining sense of loss, abandonment, shame, unworthiness, fear, anger, or mistrust will just evaporate as you fall into the most magnificent experience of divine, eternal bliss that is your birthright!

You are on Earth at this time by choice to bring in these momentous changes. You can see clearly that they are sorely needed, even if you cannot see how they can be brought about. It is God's plan that they manifest — and that means, you must admit, that they will be carried out.

Deep within you, you know that He created and is creating everything that is, and that He is infinitely loving, accepting, and forgiving. So these changes must happen. And the timing . . . well . . . it's about time, is it not?

So relax, enjoy your life, and know that the divine Creator knows what is going on. All is under perfect divine control. You came here to delight in this time . . . and you will.

ϴ ϴ ϴ

16   Much is asked of you all

Anxiety is understandable, as this is a very traumatic time in Earth's existence and therefore for everyone living a human life at this time.

Much is happening in the spiritual realms and in hidden areas of the planet that requires much energy, a lot of which is provided by those of you who intend to help with these major changes and modifications. It truly is an important watershed in the development and growth of God's magnificent divine creation, and much is asked of you all

Those of you who feel little or no sense of achievement or direction are — by your very awareness of this feeling and your intent to assist with the divine plan — helping enormously with the powerful push into the New Age of harmony, peace, delight, and abundance.

Your illnesses, dissatisfactions, anxieties, and lack of energy are caused by the enormous amounts of energy you are expending at all times in the spiritual realms. Soon this great push forward,

28

this great effort, will be completed, and your rewards will be abundant and magnificent.

Although you see so little in the way of results in spite of your enormous energy expenditure, much is truly being achieved by your powerful loving intentions. Every single one of you in prayer and meditation is providing great power and direction for the divine plan in the most appropriate manner possible.

Do not allow yourselves to be distracted and discouraged by the anger and disharmony on which the majority of your media is concentrating its attention. Give yourselves a break from it and continue to intend that all be loved, healed, and abundantly provided for, and it will be so — much sooner than you can imagine is possible.

You are all dearly loved, and your fears, anxieties, physical diseases and discomforts will very soon now be completely dissolved as your bodies and your spirits return to perfect balance and harmony.

Remember that by believing it you create it. You are here to do this, and you will achieve it. It is impossible for you to fail because you are divinely loved and protected in every moment. Just continue to intend with all your power — and your power is mighty indeed — for this stage of the divine creative endeavor to come completely and abundantly to fruition. And it will do so.

With so very much love and understanding for your difficulties that at a basic human level seem practically insoluble. . . . They are not. Peace, harmony, joy, love, wisdom, and abundance are your birthright, and very soon that will be your experience, O honored and beloved ones.

Ɵ   Ɵ   Ɵ

17   Mankind is at last awakening

Life, as you know it on Planet Earth, is moving rapidly towards a time of great change — great change in the way that you live, and in the way that you experience life as humans.

As far back as your historical records go, and way beyond that, life has been a demanding experience with much confrontation between individuals, families, tribes, and nations, leading to much suffering and very many violent deaths.

However, during the past fifty years there has been an enormous change in attitude concerning the rights and dignity of individuals and their place in society and in the world. Those who hold power over nations are no longer held in reverence and unquestioning respect, as they are increasingly called to account for their motives and behavior.

Increasing awareness of the deceptions perpetrated by so many of your elected leaders, largely due to the greatly improved systems of communication available worldwide, has led to a very strong desire and intent to change the system, so that all will be treated fairly and compassionately.

This desire and intent has led many to seek spiritual know-ledge, and to seek guidance and assistance from those in the spiritual realms — who they know exist abundantly — and who have an intense and loving desire to help when asked to do so.

The prayers and meditations of so much of humanity during the last fifty years — intending that love and compassion, peace, healing, and harmony be poured down in abundance on Planet Earth to replace the anger, fear, jealousy, and hate that have been so prevalent for so long — have been welcomed with great joy in the spiritual realms. It is seen as a strong and most definite indication that mankind is at last awakening — and awakening to accept in joy and delight the divine abundance that God intends all to experience permanently.

The abundance is there — available— awaiting your acceptance of it. It really is as simple as that.

Stop trying to work things out through the restricted reasoning of your logical linear minds. Open your hearts in acceptance of the divine energies that are poised, waiting to flow into and through you, lifting you up into full-conscious awareness of who you are and what your place and purpose is in the Creator's magnificent plan for His most dearly loved creation.

Every single one of you is totally blessed and totally loved by God, the supreme Being and Creator. So stop judging and fearing yourselves and others. Instead, open your hearts and allow the divine energy to permeate every aspect of your being. This will raise you up to a level of existence from which you will be able to see and delight in the wonder of this almighty loving creation, of which each one of you is a vital and essential part.

Each one of you — each one that has existed, exists, or will exist — is part of the divine abundance of creation that God has brought into being for His own joy and for the infinite joy of each one of you.

So open your hearts, receive His Love. Allow yourselves to be booster stations on the divine Love Grid, as His energy pours into you and through you to all of creation in an integrated flow of pure harmonious joy and abundance in every moment of existence.

Open up, allow, release your resistance to the divine energy flow, and experience existence as God has always intended you to, with infinite joy, wonder, and bliss in every moment — always and forever.

18   The intent for a peaceful environment on Earth is having a tremendous effect

Your prayers, meditations, and your intent to do the divine Will are having an effect; and you are, as you are aware, relaxing and allowing. This is all you have to do to bring divine guidance clearly into your lives.

Listen to your inner knowing, to what your heart center is telling you; and what you desire to do — what you have become human to do — will become apparent. Listen to your heart in every moment as it guides you to live with honesty and integrity at all times, so that at all times you are doing the divine Will, as God and you intend. This will bring you a sense of peace and satisfaction, and will assist those with whom you interact to find their own peace, enabling them to know their true desires, which will then lead them towards the intent to do their Father's Will.

As more and more humans meditate and pray for guidance, and for peace and harmony worldwide, the divine flow of energy to the planet intensifies as the Creator adds His energy to that of each one of you making that intent. The energy and intent for a peaceful and harmonious environment on Earth is strengthening every day with tremendous effect.

Peace on Earth will be brought about as a result of your prayerful meditations, enormously strengthened and intensely focused by the energy that God adds to your own intent.

A most beautiful, harmonious environment has been divinely planned for Planet Earth, which will enable humanity to live in permanent peace and joy. And the moment for this most wonderful change in attitude by the vast majority of humanity is rapidly approaching.

Your Creator sees your suffering and anger and is working

with you to help you release it. He loves all of you with a great intensity, and wants you to live with love and joy in your hearts at all times. He truly wants you to be singing and dancing in ecstatic delight. And because that is His Will as well as yours, it will come to pass.

You have all waited and suffered for far too long, and finally you are deciding that enough is enough, as is demonstrated by the rapidly increasing volume of prayer and meditation focused on this intent that you are generating.

Your prayers are being heard and answered. So allow yourselves to continue relaxing, and let your love for your Creator, for yourselves, and for each other fill your hearts. And let anger, fear, and distrust simply dissolve into the great ocean of Love that your prayers and your Father's divine energy is creating in every moment.

$$\ominus \quad \ominus \quad \ominus$$

19   You were created in the divine image

As you wait in eager anticipation for the momentous occasion on which humanity will burst forth from the mist and fog into the brilliant light of full consciousness, take time to allow yourselves the freedom to be truly yourselves. So many of you live behind masks or facades because you are afraid that who you really are is unacceptable, flawed, damaged, or in some other way inadequate. This is most definitely not so!

You were created in the divine image that is perfection itself. Then, with the assistance of your spiritual family you chose a human existence that would provide you with the lessons and opportunities that you wished to understand and experience.

Our Divine Destiny

The person that you are is precisely the person that — *with divine guidance* — you chose to be.

Allow that person to be fully present in every moment. When you release the fear of being seen for who you really are, you will find yourself free — wholly free — to enjoy to the full the life you have chosen to experience.

You will be filled with confidence and self-respect, and you will find yourself accepting and respecting others as you would have them accept and respect you. This will bring you joy and satisfaction, encouraging you to open your heart and allow God to fill it to overflowing with an abundance of His Love, leading you to unconditional love of all those with whom you interact. Others will respond most positively to you when they experience your acceptance of them and will then start to open their hearts, allowing the Creator's infinite Love to flow in and strengthen their confidence in their own sense of self.

And as more and more of you put away your masks and show yourselves to be the divine beings that God, in His infinite Wisdom created, His boundless Love will sweep through you, filling you with a vivid awareness of your eternal connection to Him.

It will be a grand awakening into awareness of God's Love for His creation and for all humanity. It is the most wonderfully appropriate preparation you could make for your imminent return to full consciousness, and will bring you great joy as you begin to appreciate the vastness of this ocean of Love that is racing across the Earth, enveloping all in its path. And all are in its path!

Ө   Ө   Ө

20   It is difficult for you to imagine an existence completely without cares

Many things of great importance for Planet Earth and her inhabitants are happening 24/7, as you would say. Tremendous preparations, which have been going on for some time, are almost complete, and will be completed perfectly and at the precisely appointed divine moment to usher in the new Golden Age of peace, harmony, and abundance. It truly is almost upon you. Your impatience as you wait for its arrival is most understandable — and your waiting is almost over.

So rapidly will the great changes (spiritual, social, cultural, and religious) happen across the planet that you will be left quite breathless with wonder and amazement. The divine Creator's presence is apparent in every aspect of the lives of those who choose to be aware of it; but the changes that are about to occur will jolt all of humanity into an extremely intense awareness of God's all-powerful, beneficent Presence.

It will be most wonderful to behold humanity's delighted awe-struck amazement, as the fantastic changes that bring it out of its state of spiritually lethargic existence into startling clarity and awareness envelop the planet with great rapidity at the moment God has chosen for this ecstatic event. The pain, fear, shame, and anxiety that have plagued humanity for so long will just evaporate, to seem more like the remnants of a bad dream — which is basically what they are — than the very substantial realities to which you have been accustomed for so long.

It is difficult for most of you to imagine an existence completely without cares or worries, as most of you have spent lifetimes plagued with all kinds of unwanted and apparently insoluble concerns. Their sudden removal will leave you feeling as though you are floating, as the burden they had been causing dissolves. Moreover, you will find yourselves with abundant energy and with infinite opportunities to use and enjoy it.

You will have the exuberance of small children, but without the frequent need to collapse and recoup your energy, as you will have boundless stamina. The only reason to rest will be because the idea appeals to you, but you will no longer need to.

Your sense of freedom and energy will be unbounded, so that everything you choose to do will totally delight you in every moment. This will be a truly dynamic age, releasing enormous amounts of creativity, so that all that you can imagine will seem to be possible — and it will be.

So prepare yourselves for boundless excitement in this rapidly approaching age of divine peace and abundance, in which colors, tastes, fragrances, and sounds are experienced with a previously unimagined intensity. It is your Creator's intent and desire that you experience life in this far, far richer way. And so you shall — soon.

Θ   Θ   Θ

21   Earth's place in the divine plan is absolutely pivotal

As I have been telling you for some time now, great changes to your environment and to your way of living are in the process of coming to fruition. The lives that humans live on Earth will become dramatically different: simpler, happier, far more meaningful and satisfying.

The Creator's long-term plan for Planet Earth is incredibly complex and most beautiful. The whole physical environment worldwide will be renewed and returned to the state of shimmering beauty in which it was created. At the same time the attitude of humanity towards the planet will alter as it takes up its long-forgotten role of guardian and protector. The times of desecration and abuse will be forever terminated, as all of you learn to care for and delight in the magnificence of this abundant and generous world that has supported you for so long.

Earth's place in the divine plan of creation is absolutely pivotal, because it will become, among other things, a meeting-place where many sentient beings from throughout creation will come together to discuss and plan with the Creator Himself the ongoing creative endeavor for this section of this universe.

You really have absolutely no idea at all of the vastness, beauty, and complexity of God's divine creation. But during the coming months, as all the preparations fall into place and your level of conscious awareness opens up and expands, you will begin to experience in the most marvelous and joyful way some of the amazing possibilities that He has provided within creation for the delight of all.

Activities that could not even be imagined at your present level of almost being conscious will become available for your enjoyment. Activities that up until now you have been engaging in with excitement and enthusiasm will most definitely lose their appeal as you become aware of the amazing possibilities opening up before you as you move into full consciousness. Relax, hope, trust, and enjoy for that is what you are on Earth to do.

Θ   Θ   Θ

22 Where you are is precisely where you are meant to be

As you know, every single human is a part, a reflection, an aspect of the divine Creator. And at the same time each human is a unique individual in his own right.

Each one chose to experience the human condition and incarnated fully prepared, with all the appropriate gifts, blessings, and skills necessary for their chosen life path. Every single one of you has everything you need to follow your life path with complete success to its chosen conclusion. Every event or opportunity that occurs has been planned and provided for perfectly, so worry and anxiety are not only unnecessary but also distracting. Live always in the "now" moment — in the present — right now.

What has happened is over — finished — and the future is not with you yet, so you cannot do anything about it.

As each piece of the future arrives, perfectly on schedule, it becomes "now", and you can attend to it appropriately. Worrying about it before it arrives prevents you from living fully in the present, which is what, at the center of your being, you always intend.

Live now — in full awareness — and truly take pleasure and satisfaction in the life that you planned for yourself, with such great care, great wisdom, and great love. It is what you have always intended. So, do not short-change yourself but live life to the full in every moment, by being yourself in every moment.

"Who am I?" you may ask. And this is a good question with which you should spend much time.

After asking it, allow it to percolate through you, into you, around you, without attempting to answer it by thinking about it logically with your mind. Just allow it to hang . . . and inklings, sensations, feelings, and intuitive responses will seep into your awareness.

The more you cherish the question and allow it to develop, the more you will start to become "you", letting go of the various images or cloaks that you have been wearing in an attempt to find your identity. You will find yourself just by "being", as opposed to being "someone who. . . ." You will know yourself and experience yourself, and at the same time experience yourself as All That Is. You will not be able to describe it in words, because what you are is far too vast and complicated to be described in such a limited and primitive way. You are vast beyond your ability to imagine, while also remaining within the limits you have imposed on yourself by choosing to become human.

Deep, very deep within yourself, you know this, which is why you always have hope, and why you experience an inchoate longing — a yearning for a sense of your divine connection.

You can refuse to acknowledge it, looking only at the human condition and pretending that there is nothing else. And if you do this intensely enough it can lead you to contemplate and even commit suicide. So allow your deep inner knowing of your divinity to float to the surface of your awareness, as has always been your intent. Embrace it, and enjoy the life you are living as a human, knowing — truly knowing with every cell and fiber of your being — that where you are is precisely where you are meant to be and precisely where you want to be, because that is exactly how you planned it.

When you do this, your direction and your responsiveness to life in every moment becomes clear. You no longer feel a need to justify yourself to yourself, or to others. You just "are", perfect in every moment. And with this knowledge — being yourself in every moment — all need for judgment falls away as you see that the divine Will is being done — everywhere — always.

There is no need, no requirement to set about doing the divine Will; it is being done at all times, everywhere, because the Divine is everywhere, is All That Is, doing Its Will at all times. And you are part of that — an essential and eternal part or expression of that.

As you grow more and more into awareness of that — and you cannot avoid doing so — you will live with increasing joy in every moment.

So allow it to happen. Open up and allow that divine awareness to float to the surface of your consciousness.

Then awaken into the happiness that is your God-given right.

Θ   Θ   Θ

23   You all have guides and angels most willing to help

As you proceed along the path of life that you designed with great care and much help before you incarnated, you undergo numerous experiences of an unpleasant or painful nature. Due to your state of limited consciousness as humans, you spend a lot of time wondering about these experiences and questioning their usefulness and fairness.

Frequently, it seems to you that others (whom you may well have judged and found wanting) seem to lead charmed lives when compared with your own. Then you start to wonder how God could treat you so harshly (that is, if there is a God!). So you turn from the spiritual and immerse yourselves more fully in the world of limited consciousness, leading to further dissatisfaction and pain.

But it really does not have to be like that. At all times you have guides and angels ready and most willing to help you, if you will only ask — but with intent and sincerity. Having asked, you must listen.

Listening takes much practice — if you are to hear and then understand what you hear.

If you go out into the countryside you may hear the tumultuous sounds of birdsong, or you may not notice them at all. And it is very similar with your spiritual guidance: the noise of constant thoughts in your mind frequently drowns out the quiet guidance that is offered.

Most of you have spent time with people who talk but do not

listen, even though they ask you questions. They do not hear your answers because they are so busy talking. Your spiritual guides often have the same problem with you!

 You therefore need to practice listening, and this is what true relaxation and meditation are all about. Sit comfortably and relax your body. You may need to scan it from head to toe, or vice versa, positively intending to relax each area as you scan it. Then relax your mind, switching off the thought processes by focusing softly on something beautiful in your surroundings — maybe the sky and clouds, or the landscape if you are out of doors; a vase of flowers, a blank wall, or a candle if you are indoors. Be sure to observe them without judgment: "oh, the grass needs cutting," or "I must change the wall color." Just relax and be present — maybe noticing your breathing, for example, or how comfortable or uncomfortable your body feels. Just notice, be aware. That is all.

You need to practice this relaxing into awareness regularly; and slowly you make space available for your guides to contact you in that quiet area of your self, where thought and judgment have slowed right down. If you want help — an answer to a question, for instance — ask briefly, and then sit quietly listening, waiting peacefully, with no sense of urgency.

Intuitive answers or responses will occur to you, which you can consider and develop. Eventually you will find yourself engaging in a dialogue with your guides, as opposed to asking them a repetitive set of questions that you rush to answer yourself.

If you paint, write, or play a musical instrument, you have probably experienced, from time to time, a flow of ideas which come out of nowhere when you have become totally absorbed in your creative endeavor. It could also happen with a business you are running creatively; ideas just occur to you. And so it is with spiritual guidance; you relax and allow, and ideas flow into your awareness like flashes of insight, or something just feels "right."

It does require regular daily practice to get the ideas flowing smoothly and clearly. Initially, when you start to make contact with your guides, the flow can be erratic and sporadic. It is rather like starting a fitness program: at first your muscles complain and you tire easily. As you become fitter, your muscles work happily and much more smoothly, for longer periods.

If you get out of your routine and stop exercising for a while, it can be difficult to get restarted, especially when you remember how easy it was while you were fit, and as your muscles object once more. Prayer and meditation are similar: if you slip out of your routine for any length of time, it can be difficult to re-establish it. You may even become judgmental, decide that it is not working for you, and strongly resist restarting.

However, deep within yourself, you truly know that if you make the effort you will get back into your routine, and that you will be very glad that you did so. Do not hesitate to ask for abundant help to get you started or restarted on your spiritual path, and you will be powerfully assisted.

Prayer is basically talking to God, or your guides, and asking for help.

Relaxation is just that: de-tensing and de-stressing your body so that it is comfortable and does not distract you.

And meditation is being totally quiet, without thought, allowing your guidance to flow easily and intuitively. Thoughts will of course occur, but pay them no attention. Simply return your awareness to what you were softly focusing on.

When you are in the appropriate state, you feel peaceful, quite at ease, and yet aware of your surroundings without being distracted by them, alert but relaxed. It is a most comfortable and satisfying state to settle into. Allow it to happen to you.

Ѳ   Ѳ   Ѳ

24   Love is contagious

The life that a human leads follows a path of opportunities and learning-experiences of incredible complexity. It has been designed with the assistance of many wonderful, loving guides and the wise cooperation of many other souls who are to be a part of the same incarnational group.

No human is alone on Earth, even though many may experience that sensation. Every one of you is spiritually connected to a group — family, friends, foes, work associates — with whom various interactions will occur during Earth life. And this path is approved and blessed by our divine Creator. There are no accidents or coincidences. Every occurrence and every opportunity that you experience during Earth life has been prepared or allowed for before you incarnated. But, on Earth, with your free will, you decide how to respond in every moment to each situation in which you find yourself.

You can of course seek assistance from anyone with whom you are in contact on the Earth plane — and also of course from the many guides available to each of you in the spiritual realms. But the choice whether to respond lovingly, or allow a knee-jerk reaction to occur, is entirely your decision and responsibility. Remember that not making a choice or a decision is most definitely a decision — your decision — for which you are wholly responsible.

Your decisions, or lack of them, most definitely affect others in the Earth plane, but they too made conscious, divinely guided decisions to take part in the game of life.

As I have said before, there are no victims, but on the Earth plane you can hurt each other very badly. The situations and circumstances in which you could do this were preplanned, but how you would respond was not. You are free to cause damage — or not. And only you can change yourself. You cannot change anyone else; and no one else can change you. Responding to violence with violence, anger with anger, or hate with hate, only strengthens and feeds the disharmony between you. You can do this for as long as you wish, but you will eventually learn to love.

When you start to love, the cycle changes. Love is infectious and ineradicable, and it will spread to all of humanity.

But why wait for others to bring it about when you can begin today to change your life forever? When you truly love unconditionally you are impregnable! Yes, you can still experience pain and disappointment, but living in love, with love for all, you are undefeatable. And love gives you the strength to bear any pain, and that again strengthens the love. Unconditional love is infinitely powerful. It is divine. It is your heritage and your inheritance — and you will receive it. So why not accept it now, and share it and spread it everywhere, and be in joy— always — and bring joy to every situation in which you find yourself.

Try it . . . now. It really does work! It is your Creator's gift to you, and all you have to do is open your heart and say "yes" to Him. He longs for you to do this because He knows what happiness it will bring you.

Don't just pay it lip service. Embrace it wholly and experience the joy it will bring you.

Θ Θ Θ

25 Your bodies are adjusting themselves in readiness for the big change

The final preparations for the big changes are going very well indeed, as this stage rapidly draws towards its conclusion. You do not have much longer to wait until you experience the marvels that your Creator has prepared for you.

As you wait during these last few days, your spiritual aspects are becoming increasingly active in preparation for all to unfold. You will feel strange sensations from time to time as your various energy fields prepare themselves for unification. You may experience moments of euphoria, alternating with moments of intense anxiety, as these fields adjust themselves in readiness for the change. The way they will operate after the change will be very different from the way to which you have been accustomed, and so certain preparatory measures have to be taken in advance.

You will feel this in your bodies as intestinal rumblings, indigestion, muscular twitching and aches, and an increase in your need for sleep, as you will tire more easily than normal. Do not be concerned about it; it is part of the necessary preparations your bodies need to make so that they can cope easily and efficiently with their new mode of being after the big changes.

The fact that you are feeling all this, becoming aware of it, is an indication of how close the big event is. Just relax and enjoy life as this stage of your existence draws to a close to allow the new Golden Age to be ushered in with a multitude of celebrations.

ϴ ϴ ϴ

26 Free will is so misunderstood by humanity

Free will is so misunderstood by humanity! It is there for your benefit only, and it is your individual power to use as you see fit. And yet so many of you give away that power to others, and refuse to make your own decisions.

Others are incapable of using your power for your good. Only you can do that. But they can and do use your power — by manipulating you, and a very large majority of your fellows. So do not give it away!

Every individual has his own power of will and does not need anyone else's. Using the power belonging to another (e.g. making another's decisions for him) can harm not only that individual but also the one using it.

The power of your free will is personally customized; it truly has no resale value. But for you its power is limitless. However far you want to go — grow — it will be with you: drawing you on, strengthening your intent, encouraging you to continue, pointing out the way. The more you use it, the more in tune with it you become. The possibilities are limitless. Any limits you meet, you have set for yourself.

Life is frequently confusing for you at present as you break free from the restrictions imposed on you by your cultures, religions, and education. These have put you where you most definitely do not want to be: boxed up in a prison of restrictive ideas and beliefs that you were told not to question. You were led to believe, moreover, that to question them was disloyal, unworthy, distrustful, and unacceptable; in fact, almost an act of betrayal!

Doubts naturally arose in your consciousness which you quickly repressed, as you were afraid that to acknowledge them would put you in severe conflict with your parents and other authority figures in your life. Who you thought you were and what you felt became increasingly frightening and unacceptable, and the older you became the more you believed that that essence of you, which you were repressing, was somehow inadequate, sinful, or unacceptable in an environment in which obedience and conformity seemed essential for survival.

Over the years, as you learned to see the insanity of the environmental culture in which you were raised, the conflict within you became increasingly vociferous as your awareness increased and your conditioning continued to attempted to shut it down. You are torn between loyalty on the one hand, to an imposed and unreasonable system to which you feel you owe a lot, and on the other, to an awareness of the inhumanity and dishonesty of it and your need to break free. And you fear that to change means discarding everything and starting over.

The idea of starting over brings unpleasantly to mind the fear and trauma you experienced in early life and, more intensely, the insecurity and and anxiety you experienced as you grew through childhood and adolescence when you were frequently made to feel unacceptable. Needless to say, you do not wish to go through all that again!

But starting over is not required; nor is discarding anything of value that you have learned. What you need to do is open up and allow new experiences of your own choosing to flow into your life, because that is what life is for. You no longer need to accept imposed values or experiences, and furthermore, there is no need for fear and anxiety as punishment and disapproval are not waiting to pounce! The only approval or disapproval that has any validity is your own, but be sure that your assessment is unencumbered by cultural overlays and judgments.

So open up, stand back, and observe and enjoy your freedom

as you allow yourself to experience your choices in every area of your life. Try to become aware of self-censure and release it. You are what you are meant to be, and that is much vaster, more powerful, and more glorious than you can possibly imagine!

Θ   Θ   Θ

27 Many on Earth have become lost in the dream state

As you are well aware, to be fully conscious is your divine heritage. An Earth life as a human is an opportunity to experience a far less spiritually evolved way of living, and to bring the two together in divine harmony. However, many on Earth have become lost in the dream state with which an earthly existence attempts to seduce them, and they need assistance and encouragement to awaken.

It is as though they were lost in an enormous maze of labyrinthine proportions and, while it is their intention to find their way out, as they know full well they can, they keep being distracted by the events taking place in the various environments through which they pass on their way to the exit.

To live on Earth as a human is indeed a difficult and demanding undertaking, as the many distractions and illusions an Earth life provides are very confusing, making the call to awaken hard to hear. Nevertheless, as more and more of you do start to awaken, you in turn assist others to do likewise. And so the process of awakening is proceeding most satisfactorily and accelerating rather rapidly.

You are beginning to realize that there is a far, far better way to experience life, namely, by living consciously, and at all times being in the state of awareness and knowledge that that is God's infinite and all-enveloping mantle of unconditional acceptance and love.

The intense dream state, which an earthly existence attempts to seduce you into believing is the only possible state of existence, is something that you have created for yourselves over eons of time, as you experience it. Consequently, it appears to be not only totally real, but also the only reality possible. This vast misperception seems to provide an enormous environment, centered on Planet Earth, and stretching forever in all directions, forming what you describe as the "universe."

Within this universe, and as your scientists' knowledge increases and they "discover" the laws that control it, there seems to be no end to the territories available for mankind to explore, conquer, and then use for its own rather shallow ends, including perhaps somewhere to dump the growing quantities of highly toxic waste that are an ongoing result of your inability to act responsibly as guardians and protectors of your planet.

The damage being done to Earth in the name of great scientific progress is itself acting as a wake-up call for many who, as they turn their attention increasingly towards preventing further damage and attempting to repair that which has already occurred, are starting to find within themselves evidence of a spiritual design and purpose, a divine connection that is permanent and ineradicable.

It is both a shock and a joy. And it is this discovery within yourselves that is, as divinely planned and intended, creating the groundswell of true spirituality that is spreading rapidly throughout the planet and ensuring that all will awaken, and in a timely and expeditious manner, so that you will very soon experience full-conscious awareness of your divine heritage, to which you are permanently connected but which you had temporarily forgotten. The permanent state of infinite joy and happiness that this state of existence provides will dissolve the mists and madnesses of the dream state to which you have been clinging so ferociously for so long.

Θ   Θ   Θ

28   ... And you will awaken

The process of awakening into God's divine Reality can seem slow and arduous. But keep reminding yourselves that you are truly home there, always, and that you will awaken, and that your joy and delight will be wonderful and utterly beyond any happiness you can even imagine experiencing in this illusory non-reality that presently seems so real to you.

It is an illusion you have all agreed to create and to cooperate in maintaining. However, deep within each of you is the knowledge that this existence you are experiencing so intensely is indeed make-believe.

You know that you are always in the divine Presence, because there is nowhere else, and that you will become disillusioned enough to awaken from this unreality into the only Reality, which is Oneness with God — where you always are.

God's Love for His creation — you — is beyond description or imagination. It can only be experienced. You are experiencing it now, but by your own choice you are limiting your experience to that of the totally unsatisfactory dream state in which it appears to you that you are living.

Without God there would be nothing — absolutely nothing — and that is impossible because God is!

The reality you are experiencing is a very unsatisfactory and confusing dream, and without God that experiencing would be impossible, because there would be no one to experience it, no sensations, and nothing to know. Therefore, because you are dreaming, God exists. And because God exists, your dream is an extremely limiting experience that is completely imaginary.

You are living in the most magnificent and perfect, divine Reality and have chosen to be totally unaware of it.

Your unawareness will dissolve and disintegrate, and you will awaken with joy and wonder into the only possible reality: God's divine Reality that is All That Is. And it will be complete, and so will you, while your illusion will be gone forever, having never in fact existed. It was a mind game that you have closed, terminated, and wholly forgotten.

And all that remains is All That Is, always, eternally — in perfect, divine, perpetual, exquisite bliss.

Θ   Θ   Θ

29   Life is a demanding task

Life as a human is not an experience you chose to undergo lightly. It is a demanding task, and much prior thought and planning went into it to ensure that you understood fully the enormous challenge you were undertaking.

At all times during your human existence, you have guides ready, willing, and able to assist you, should you ask for help. However, the vast majority of you have enormous difficulty in remembering that you have only to call on them to receive assistance instantly. And those of you who do remember and ask, have trouble tuning in to them.

To spend many quiet moments every day, releasing yourselves from your thoughts so that their communication, guidance, and assistance can be heard and experienced is most important.

A Saul Book

Thought, while very necessary for the satisfactory operation of your human lives, is generally quite distracting from and detrimental to your spiritual lives. Both occur simultaneously (you experience the two concurrently), but it is the human aspect of which you are most conscious, because it is so noisy and because you identify so strongly with it through your bodily needs.

Part of the reason you chose to be human was so that you could learn to integrate the two and put that learning into constant practice. Quiet periods of reflection and meditation are the way to achieve that. When you still your mind, you make space to hear, to be aware of your inner spiritual knowing, and allow your guides to communicate with you, if that is your wish.

The more space you make available in your life for your spiritual side to grow and develop, the more balanced and peaceful you become, as your human (physical) aspect integrates more and more fully with your spiritual aspect. The two are, of course, one and the split or separation is really illusory, as the one cannot exist without the other, although one (the spiritual) may seem to be a sleeping-partner, existing almost imperceptibly in the background.

To operate fully consciously as a human, both aspects need to be balanced. If they are not, you drift towards one of the weighted ends, either totally of the world, or totally of the spirit. When you live like this — and most people do — judgment comes in, advising you that the aspect towards which you are disinclined is inappropriate, and as you move away from it the strength and intensity of the judgment grows, and so does your lack of balance.

This is why those who are either completely worldly or completely spiritual cannot and do not wish to communicate with each other, for they see the others as being in error, wasting their lives, and best dismissed. These two extremes are in a sense identical; their perceptions merely appear to be different because they are looking in opposite directions!

Those towards the middle are more balanced, can see both points of view, can communicate with either, and enjoy doing so.

When you are balanced, you are effectively on the mountain top with a clear view in all directions, seeing the big picture, and able to value all the small pieces that go to make it up. When you are at one end of the scale, unbalanced, you are in a very small valley from which you cannot see out. Occasionally, however, things fall in on top of you, frightening and threatening you!

You are here to achieve balance and integration, and you arrived with all the tools necessary to do the job. So make the space many times each day to do this, by relaxing, quieting your mind, and inviting your guides and your higher self to help you . . . and they will.

You will be amazed at the speed with which you will see improvements in your life experience as you allow your spiritual and physical integration to take place.

Θ   Θ   Θ

30 Whatever happens — anywhere — is always divinely intended

The path that each human has chosen to experience is indeed most carefully planned, so that all the experiences that the entity wishes to explore in a lifetime are always presented at the most appropriate moment. Everything that happens to or around an individual during his life has been willingly planned in advance in order to achieve the maximum value and spiritual growth in the time available.

God provides everything an entity requires (love, healing, compassion, acceptance, forgiveness, opportunities, and experiences) in loving abundance so that nothing is ever wasted, and there are no leftovers!

Everything that is so abundantly provided always fulfills its divinely directed purpose, although of course this is frequently not apparent to those experiencing the physical realm.

Whatever happens — anywhere — is always divinely *intended*, and due to humanity's very restricted awareness and very limited ability to see the big picture, God's Intent on the physical realm can seem harsh, cruel, and unloving. But you must remember that with divine and loving guidance each one of you chose your unique, wonderful — yes, truly wonderful — and individual life paths in full knowledge and understanding, in order to achieve results that you can only realize through a human life.

It is the limited viewpoint that you chose as humans to experience that presents you with a perception of pain, disaster, and catastrophe in so many areas of the planet. Yet the most wonderful growth that these events create and encourage are truly marvelous to behold, and will give you great joy when you return to your inheritance in the spiritual realms.

While you remain in the physical realm, you are provided with an abundance of Love, compassion, healing, and guidance, which you will experience if you open your hearts in acceptance. When you do this, you receive the strength to cope in situations that would otherwise seem intolerable. Acceptance of the situation then leads to a sense of trust and a calm and peaceful knowing that all manner of things will truly be well — an awareness that the situation that is perceived in human terms as intensely painful will, like bad weather, pass away, leaving behind a cleansed and sparkling environment that is most uplifting to experience!

Θ   Θ   Θ

31 Deep within, you know that your future will be absolutely magnificent

God's infinite Love for His creation is utterly beyond the imaginative powers of perception of any of the conscious entities that He has created. Each entity can experience it to the extent that its limited perception can accept and allow; and for each entity the experience is different.

As the entity grows and develops spiritually, its ability to experience the infinite divine Love of the Creator expands. The entity's spiritual growth never ceases; it is eternally ongoing, and so therefore is its ability to experience divine Love ever ongoing and expanding. The wonder and the bliss continue eternally to grow and increase, forever amazing and delighting. And yet it is totally beyond wonder.

When humans return finally to the spiritual realms, having completed all their human experiences, their amazement and delight is most exquisite for us to behold. They are also shocked to recall the intensity with which they were able to doubt God's infinite Love for them and His infinite acceptance of them.

When all becomes clear to the newly returned and reawakened soul, her bliss, her unbridled delight and happiness are, as we have already noted, completely beyond anything she could have imagined.

If your imaginations gave you more than the tiniest inkling of what to expect, it would be impossible for you to complete the tasks you set yourselves before you incarnated as humans.

Deep within you, you know that your reward, your future, will indeed be magnificent, but that knowledge has to remain concealed — and yet, in a way, known (quite a paradox!) — so that the soul may successfully complete her human experience without distractions that are inappropriate to the task at hand.

This deep inner knowing provides strength and courage to enable the human entity to follow her path, allowing her wisdom to expand continuously. Following her path, whatever the apparent setbacks, disappointments, and pains she experiences, is the most appropriate way to move forward spiritually and to grow steadily into into a profound awareness of God's existence and of His Love for her.

On a three-dimensional level, it often seems that the pain, unfairness, disappointments, and the sense of total abandonment are beyond unbearable. Extremely painful . . .yes! Unbearable . . . no.

You will come through this, and when you do, you will know that what you are receiving as your reward — your God-given right — was absolutely worth every moment of pain and suffering, even if it was magnified many thousands of times

When you return to that place that you have never left — Oneness with God — the memory of your pain will be quite removed; you will never have suffered it. You will see that it really was an illusion, while your bliss and happiness have been an unbroken, continuous experience from the moment of your creation.

Yes, this is difficult to believe and impossible to understand, but it is true. And very soon you will experience this wonder and this bliss. So hang in there . . .

Ө   Ө   Ө

32   The direction of your life path may change as your spiritual vision becomes clearer

As you journey through life and accept — with love — the lessons it has to teach you, wonderful things happen: you become increasingly aware that life is fun and enjoyable in every situation; that it truly is abundantly creative in every moment; and that even when events that would previously have angered, frightened, or hurt you occur, you will find that these feelings and emotions are far less intense. You will be aware of the bigger picture around these events (but not in any great detail), and that will enable you to know that they have a purpose and a meaning for all involved in them, which will lead on to greater spiritual awareness and peace, in proportion to the degree of openness and love with which they are accepted.

At a higher level, all truly know that they agreed to incarnate at this particular time and that there is a very definite purpose and intent to their lives, even though at the level at which you experience existence as humans, it is not at all clear what this purpose is.

Nevertheless, it does give you a strong desire to seek it out and identify it, although frequently a misidentification occurs, and people can lock on to a purpose that is not really appropriate.

If you can remain open of heart and mind as you search to identify your life's purpose, you will find that, in human terms, it is a constantly changing purpose. Each experience in your life can teach you something which will assist you on your journey of spiritual growth and development — if you will permit it.

That is how you planned your life path before you incarnated, and with each spiritual lesson learned, the love and wisdom within you is nourished, and so grows and intensifies. This allows you to see more clearly what your life is about, and so the purpose and direction of your life path may change as your spiritual vision becomes clearer.

If you look back over your life, you will perceive the goals for which you were aiming — some achieved, some not — and you will remember that when you set some of the major ones, it seemed at the time that achievement of them would mark the culmination and fulfillment of your life. However, when you achieved them, or changed them, you discovered that further aiming-points lay ahead of you, encouraging you onwards.

To be aware at the start of your human existence of what you truly aspired to achieve when you planned your life would be very discouraging for you as a human, because your goal would appear to be beyond the bounds of possibility.

As you achieve or discard goals during your life, appropriate new ones appear, leading you on. The new ones that appear will depend on which of the previous ones you achieved or discarded, making the path ahead very difficult to foresee for more than a very short way.

You are like an explorer in a foreign land: you set out in a certain direction with intent and purpose, but obstacles and difficulties occur which make it necessary for you to adjust or actually change your plan. However, the intricacy and brilliance of the planning of your original life path ensures that whatever adjustments are made, the traveler will be presented with the most spiritually rewarding choices in any given situation.

ϴ   ϴ   ϴ

33   You are all divine flames of intense brilliance and beauty

Humanity is in the process of returning to full consciousness — a process that has been ongoing since its creation.

This process is constantly accelerating and will continue to do so as more and more of you become aware that you have a permanent , eternal, divine heritage. It provides you easily and swiftly with all that you need for existence, because you are all constantly connected in every moment to the divine Creator that many of you call God.

The Creator is a continuous outpouring of Love, Grace, and Creative Energy — the life force. And all that exists is continually and permanently connected to that abundant and ever-expanding ocean of creative potential and has the power and the ability to develop it as it chooses.

Every one of you is part of that; you always have been, and you will always continue to be, in the divine instant that is the ever-present now.

In your human condition — a condition each one of you has chosen to experience for the wonderful lessons it makes available to you — your amnesia concerning who you really are does make it quite difficult to connect consciously with the fullness, the magnificence of what you really are: divine flames of intense brilliance and beauty, which is clearly apparent to all in the spiritual realms. You will come to recognize, identify with, and experience your true nature, and at the deepest, most spiritual level of your many levels of existence you are constantly aware of your true divine nature.

To live on Earth as a human is to participate in the ongoing process to bring all aspects of your existence — and you have many — into balance and harmony with the One, God, All That Is. And at times it does seem like an impossible and incomprehensible task that you have set yourselves.

Nevertheless, this most definitely is not the case; everything you need to complete your permanent reconnection with the deeply harmonious and blissful Reality that is All That Is, is available to you right now, and so is all the assistance you could possibly desire to help you achieve that state of being.

God wants you to reconnect. He intends you to reconnect, and He is constantly providing everything you need to do so. You will reconnect!

Ask to reconnect, intend to reconnect, and allow yourselves to reconnect. Release all judgment of yourselves and others. Release all shame, all guilt, all fear, all sense of unworthiness, and be the magnificent beings of brilliant beauty and light that you are. That is how you were created; that is what you eternally are.

Believe it . . . be it . . . for a state of wondrous joy is your birthright.

θ θ θ

34 Compassion will flower within humanity

As the spiritual growth of humanity proceeds for many at a

greatly accelerated pace, many will find themselves in intensely demanding situations where they seemingly have neither the wisdom nor the restraint to cope adequately, harmoniously, or rationally, and in which they may well find themselves reacting angrily at the time, only to regret their reaction later, when they come to reflect on it. And frequently in their reflecting, seeing errors that they have made, they will become angry with themselves. Too often anger at self is unacceptable, and so it is projected outwards, at others or at circumstances, creating an increase in the energies of anger swirling around them.

If people could see that the anger they are projecting often starts with anger at self, and could stop at that point and forgive themselves, the creation of anger energies would decrease phenomenally, greatly assisting the peaceful energies that all truly desire to have grow and flourish.

When you meditate, reflect, or pray, it is very good and helpful to send out the intent that people may recognize and forgive their anger at themselves, because forgiving and accepting themselves is an essential first step on the road to forgiving others. Intend for all people to realize that they are indeed divine creations of the divine Creator, that they are totally acceptable and totally forgiven, and that all they need to do is to accept themselves, knowing that they are truly one in harmonious union with the Divine.

As they learn to accept themselves, releasing the imposed feelings of unacceptability that they have been harboring and nurturing, their feelings of anger and resentment will melt away, and they will find that they no longer need to judge and condemn others, because they realize that those others are also beautiful, divine creations who, like themselves, have been damaged and are in pain.

As more and more of you do this, compassion will flower within humanity, enabling forgiveness and healing to replace the anger and judgment, which are all too prevalent in so many environments.

ϴ ϴ ϴ

35 You are totally acceptable just the way you are

As you grow and develop spiritually, life becomes more enjoyable, more peaceful, more relaxed, and more natural. Like a mature tree, you can stand and survey all about you without getting involved in petty goings-on, and yet remain able to observe, listen, and provide an environment that feels safe, peaceful, secure, and accepting to those in your vicinity. This produces a lovely energy that encourages and allows others to be themselves in your presence.

To be yourself when alone and unobserved is very, very different from being yourself in the presence of others. When you are alone, knowing that you are safe, you may often wonder what others would think of you if they saw you as you truly are, and perhaps you hope that they will never have that opportunity.

If, however, you find yourself in the presence of someone by whom you feel completely unthreatened, and you start to disclose the real you, and at each disclosure you find you still feel safe and accepted, you begin to move closer to self-acceptance, and even self-love, because your disclosures allow you to experience yourself as far less threatening than you had expected. You begin to discover that being you — whatever that may mean — is OK.

It is very important and most helpful for a human to find

someone to whom they can express their true feelings and beliefs, knowing that they will not be rejected or judged, and to have such a friend provides a welcome sense of security, peace, and ease. It provides him with an environment in which he can practice being himself — safely, securely, and humorously!

Yes, humor is very important to growth and development; you need to feel free to see the funny side of things, to laugh (but not to be laughed at!) and enjoy experiencing your personal voyage of self-discovery as it unfolds before you.

Discovering yourself in the presence of someone you trust is far more valuable and self-affirming than doing it alone, where you will always be left with doubts, wondering whether you are acceptable to another. Whereas in the presence of your trusted friend, you can plainly see that you are, and always will remain, completely acceptable — just the way you are.

Θ   Θ   Θ

36   The divine plan is approaching a very crucial stage

The Creator's magnificent plan for humanity is approaching a very crucial stage. And so it is imperative that those holding the Light — those who are aware that humanity is soon to move into a state of full consciousness — redouble the strength of their intent to bring this about whenever they pray or meditate. The intent and desire of those of you who are praying and meditating regularly is very powerful, and is an important aspect of God's plan.

Humanity was created in Love — to cooperate and co-create with God, as His divine plan for you all unfolds. You are an essential part of it, and your cooperation is required. You have been cooperating most beautifully, but now an even stronger and more intense period of focused intent is called for, as the culmination of this stage of the divine, creative plan approaches, which will usher in the new Golden Age of joy, abundance, and prosperity for all on Mother Earth.

When you pray and meditate, make a point of envisaging a world free of strife, anger, and torment, where these have been replaced by peace, harmony, and wise and enthusiastic cooperation, steeped in infinite love and acceptance.

This is what the new Golden Age is bringing for you all. So open your hearts in prayer and meditation to embrace it and bring it forth. It is your divine right, your divine heritage, and the Creator wants you to experience it and enjoy it fully and eternally. By strengthening your prayers and intentions to bring it to fruition, you greatly intensify the joy that it will bring you when it arrives — very soon now.

Your prayers and intentions are extremely powerful at this time and continue to increase in power, as the divine energies flood the Earth to assist in anchoring the New Age.

The moment for its arrival is very close, which is why the guiding and aligning energies for it are so strong. Use your imaginations — they are very powerful — and realize how wonderful and joyful life is about to become for you all. Creative visualization is something you are all very good at, if you will allow yourselves to be. So use this ability every time you pray and meditate, to imagine this magnificent new Golden Age that you are in the process of creating with God, for your unending peace and happiness.

θ   θ   θ

37   ... And consequently nothing can prevent it

God's perpetually developing plan for His creation is infinitely abundant, providing everything that a conscious being could possibly desire in order to live in a state of total bliss. That is His Intent, because of His infinite Love for every element of His creation.

What humanity is currently experiencing on Earth — strife, pain, repression, hunger and thirst in some areas, abundance and satiation in others — is something that each individual in those areas has chosen for the spiritual lessons they will provide. There are no accidents of birth; each human incarnates in precisely the appropriate place to experience the lessons he has chosen to undergo.

The divine energies inundating Planet Earth at this time provide every human with exactly what she needs to follow her life path and to learn and fully understand the lessons it is providing for her. All are infinitely loved by God, and all are capable of loving unconditionally. More and more of you are doing this in every moment, as you become individually aware that this is the divine Will, and that this is why you chose to be human.

Life as a human is the most wonderful opportunity to learn the lesson of unconditional love, and then to put it into practice. Many are doing this and experiencing the resulting joy and peace that that brings them. This leads them to trust completely that all is divinely intended, and that they are totally loved and protected at all times, wherever they may be. It is this phenomenal growth in the numbers of you practicing unconditional love that is moving humanity forward so rapidly towards the state of full consciousness that is your divine heritage.

The Creator's Will is always achieved precisely, as and when He intends it. And it is His Will that humanity be raised into full consciousness. More and more of you are becoming aware of this, and it provides increasing power and momentum to the drive towards this heavenly state of existence.

It is a state of existence that every human who has ever lived, lives, or will come to live, is destined to experience — eternally. And the arrival of that state of being is very close indeed.

Allow the knowledge that this is so— and that knowledge is present, deep within each of you — to come into your awareness and enjoy with eager anticipation the time remaining before the mist and fog dissolve, and you find yourselves bursting forth with wonder and amazement into this state for which you have been hoping and dreaming for so long.

It is your God-given right to live permanently and perpetually in that blissful state. And very soon you will . . . because it is the Creator's Intent that you shall. It is also your intent, and consequently nothing can prevent it. Enjoy and delight in the fact that soon you will be more fantastically and exhilaratingly alive than you can possibly imagine.

Ɵ   Ɵ   Ɵ

38   You are all priceless jewels in God's divine creation

There are many loving, generous, and open-hearted people on your beautiful planet, so make a point of making and maintaining contact with them, because networking with other loving beings spreads and intensifies the divine energies presently pouring down so abundantly on Planet Earth.

Making and maintaining contact strengthens and intensifies your hope and your faith that there is a divine plan of the utmost beauty and efficiency that is changing humanity's perception of itself and of the planet that protects and shelters it.

Soon the efforts of the many groups that meet to meditate and pray for a divine resolution to the conflicts of various sorts that plague the Earth and her inhabitants will meld and further intensify, to bring about essential changes in perception and lifestyle. The results of this vast and cooperative venture by so many loving beings on your planet will be amazing and far-reaching.

Change, which for so long has been slow and plodding, with many missteps, will take place very rapidly across the Earth, as more and more people awaken and become aware of their divine heritage. Their awakening will bring them confidence and enthusiasm, and they will be filled with happiness as they see their families, friends, foes, and neighbors also awakening.

The Creator's plan for you all is truly magnificent. The planning and preparation have been meticulous and time-consuming. Now, the moment of execution is almost upon you, as all position themselves to carry out their essential individual roles at this point in the holy master plan, as it completes another stage in its ongoing development.

There will be a wonderful celebration, a party of unexpected magnificence to which all are invited. The joy and wonder, the awe and the thrill will envelop you all in ways that you cannot possibly imagine, when God unveils Paradise for you here on Earth, as He keeps and makes good the promises He has made to you over all the eons you have been incarnating and returning to experience untold numbers of Earth lives.

You are all God's children, divinely loved, divinely cherished, priceless jewels in His divine creation. And you will each recognize and delight in the magnificence and beauty of each other, as you join in the grand display of all your talents for the enjoyment of all. And God's pleasure in your joy will be most wondrous to behold.

Θ   Θ   Θ

39   The fog that presently enshrouds you will just dissolve — all in an instant

Much is going on the spiritual realms as the moment for the vast majority of humanity to return to full consciousness approaches rapidly. In terms of numbers of souls, there are indeed many who are not yet willing to acknowledge and accept this magnif-icent, divine gift that has been so lovingly prepared by the Creator for His lovely and beloved children. However, their unwillingness and unreadiness to move into full consciousness at this moment in their spiritual evolution will not be permitted to delay that glorious occasion for all the others who have been praying and hoping for it for so long.

Those who continue to insist on the need for distrust, confrontation, and the pain and destruction that brings, will be allowed to continue on that path for as long as they need it. When they are ready to open their hearts to accept God's infinite Love, it will most certainly pour in and suffuse them completely, awakening them to the wonder of full consciousness and their divine heritage. But their desire and intent to continue following that path will not be permitted to prevent or delay the return to full consciousness of the greater majority of humans.

Full consciousness — and all that that entails — is extremely close now. Your prayers are truly heard and answered, always, in the moment that you make them; and the divine Intent that you move into that most glorious state — full consciousness of your inseparable connection to the Creator — will occur very shortly.

It has been divinely planned and intended since the dawn of time, as you call it, and it will occur precisely as planned. Your joy as you return to your natural state of oneness with your Creator is guaranteed, and it will not be delayed. In the eternal "now" moment, time, as you experience it, does not and never has existed. And even "in time" — as you are currently choosing to experience it — your return to full consciousness has not in any manner been delayed.

Your desire and intent to be, once again, fully-conscious beings, as your divine Father always intends, has been rapidly intensifying over the last few decades of your present earthly incarnation. And this has created a sense of great impatience, leading you to wonder whether His very existence is mere wishful-thinking on the part of frightened and delusional humans who do not wish to face up to the reality of an implacably impersonal universe or the termination of life at the end of a meaningless lifespan.

Deep within yourselves you truly know that this is not so! Nevertheless, you have created this illusory scenario of total abandonment, ending in death, and then . . . nothing. But that is just a game you are playing, and the outcome will be an even greater and more wonderful sense of awe, amazement, and unrestrained joy when the veils — the fog in which you have presently shrouded yourselves — dissolve, all in an instant.

Then you will find yourselves once again, fully-conscious beings, romping delightedly without inhibitions or cares in the divine pastures in which you have been playing for your whole existence, totally safe and totally connected to the divine Being, your Creator, the vast ocean of Love that is All That Is.

As I have told you repeatedly, you are continuously and eternally connected to and a part of the Creator, because no other form of existence is possible. Just relax into the absolute certainty that the divine plan is unfolding precisely as intended and that His Will for you — complete and utter happiness for all eternity — will be yours very soon indeed.

Ө Ө Ө

40 Your reawakening has truly been earned — and with flying colors

All those choosing to undergo the human experience on Planet Earth were very well aware of the difficulty of the task that they were undertaking. It was a choice made with great wisdom, knowledge, and foresight, in the absolute faith that it would be completed — magnificently and as planned — within the allotted time frame.

The Creator will not allow anything to interfere with, let alone prevent, the timely completion of this task — or for that matter with any of the many other creative endeavors that He has planned and has in progress throughout His infinite domain of solar systems, galaxies, and universes. His creative endeavors will always be completed as planned, magnificently, and on schedule.

Humans — as with all other intelligent beings throughout creation — have only to allow themselves to be a part of this enthralling experience which He has prepared for them, if they wish to come into the bliss-filled state of existence that He has made their birthright.

What we are all learning — and what we already understand at the deepest levels of our being — is that unconditional acceptance of creation, and of our oneness with it, is what intelligent life in any form is all about. However, that Oneness, in all Its myriad expressions of Itself, is forever exploring and expanding, drawing all life forms along with it in one glorious symphony of creative energy.

Acceptance leads to bliss, which leads to further acceptance, in an unending and mind-bogglingly creative expansion of consciousness into ever-growing awareness of All That Is, which in turn will continue to grow and expand infinitely and eternally.

The task that humanity has chosen to accomplish is self-acceptance, which, when completed — and that completion will be surprisingly soon — will mean that every single soul who has experienced, is experiencing, or will experience existence as a human will be raised suddenly and wonderfully into full-conscious awareness of who they truly are. The blinkers will fall from everyone's eyes, and you will all recognize in yourselves, and in every other, your true magnificence, which until that moment had been concealed from you by your own choice, so that you could experience the human state and work through the task that being human involves.

Your reawakening will be the most blissfully wonderful experience, and you have all — every one of you without exception — truly earned it with flying colors. Very soon now you will awaken and find yourselves Home, in total bliss. Continue to carry the light and hold on to your faith in God's and your infinite glory.

θ θ θ

41 Accidents and illnesses are powerful attempts to attract your attention

As your life flows along the path you create for it, you will notice many apparent coincidences occurring which enable you to further your spiritual development easily and smoothly. When you need time to relax and muse, you will find yourselves between jobs or on vacation. When you need stimulation, you will find much going on in your lives that requires your attention. You meet new people at the right moment for the relationship that you will develop with them, and when what you need to do together is completed, you will move on.

Sometimes you find yourselves wondering what it was in a friend that attracted you to him, as it seems that now you have no meeting-point. It could well be that you are attempting to prolong a relationship when its purpose has been completed.

At other times you maintain contact with people for many years even though the relationship seems to have little to offer either of you. In this case you may well be cooperating on a deep spiritual level of which you have no conscious awareness.

All relationships that occur in your lives have been arranged prior to incarnation; consequently, the coincidences that occur only appear to be coincidental. How you develop your relationships once the meeting has taken place is totally up to you. You planned a life and provided for many opportunities to occur as you progressed along its course. How you will actually respond to them is not planned in advance, and depends on your feelings and intuition. Often you may not even notice them, as they may not seem very different from the multitude of distractions that life as a human supplies.

When you start to make a positive effort to encourage the development of your spiritual aspects, you will become aware of many more of the opportunities that are available to you. It may seem that suddenly life has far more to offer you than it did before, but this is not the case — your spiritual growth has opened up your awareness, enabling you to see opportunities that previously you would have missed or discounted.

The more you develop your spiritual side, the more you open up to life, and the more life opens up to you. Your field of interests expands, and so does your ability to develop and enjoy those interests.

If you are depressed and nothing really interests you, it is a strong signal that you need to set aside a lot of your life for relaxation and meditation in order to seek assistance from the realms of spirit. Frequently, that is very difficult because depression and lack of interest feed on each other, strengthening their hold on you. Sometimes an accident or seriousness illness will occur to shake you out of your lethargy.

Accidents and illnesses are always powerful attempts to get

your attention. So respond to them positively and listen for the information that they are undoubtedly able to provide. As I have said before, all the occurrences in your lives have a deep spiritual purpose; so look out for the signals, pay attention to your lives, every aspect of them, and learn the lessons you came on Earth to learn.

When you open yourselves up to this divine flow of information and allow, assist, and encourage yourselves to respond positively to it, your energy and enthusiasm for life will expand, and you will gain a sense of peace and serenity which will be an ever-deepening joy to experience.

So listen, learn, respond, and enjoy to the full this wonderful life your Creator has provided for you in response to your request. It is yours to use and experience to the utmost. So do so . . . and in doing so, you do God's Will and your own.

Ɵ   Ɵ   Ɵ

42 Observe and allow what is happening

Life commences as activity— which increases rapidly as the life develops, leading to many valuable experiences. It then becomes necessary to learn to relax, reflect, and meditate so that understanding the meaning of it all can come into awareness.

As the life proceeds, the need for activity decreases, and that need to relax, reflect, and meditate becomes paramount. The earlier, active life experiences provide the material for the later life stage of reflection. The first stage flows naturally into the second, allowing the sense of urgency, which was the motivating energy earlier in life, to abate so that the necessary meditation and reflection can take place. Urgency and reflection are not compatible.

As the sense of urgency becomes less pressing, a soul is frequently perturbed by a sense of lack — a loss of interest in the things and activities that had held much fascination for it — and this can initially be unsettling and depressing. However, as the soul spends more time in reflection and meditation, the unsettling feelings that this lack of urgency initially caused will dissolve, leading to a sense of peace and contentment, which will allow wisdom to develop, thus completing the life cycle.

Fighting against this natural life progression is damaging for the body, which has been designed precisely for these periodic changes, and leads to illness and possible premature death. Trees are a magnificent example of this life progression, developing rapidly, urgently, and spontaneously to maturity, and then living very long lives as mature and wise entities, perfectly fulfilling their life purpose. Humanity can learn a lot from observing trees, and from tuning in to their harmonious energy vibrations.

Your meditation periods will become more fruitful as your intention to be spiritually motivated intensifies and strengthens. Meditating is like playing a musical instrument: a lot of practice is necessary before proficiency is achieved. And then continuing practice is required to maintain and improve on that proficiency.

As you progress through life and allow yourselves to experience it in all its many and varied manifestations, it becomes easier and feels very natural, just to be and to accept whatever is happening at any given moment. "What is happening" has been carefully orchestrated to fit precisely into that moment to provide the most expeditious opportunity for a person's spiritual growth at that point. It is the most appropriate event that could be experienced at that moment, and the trick is to allow it and to observe it so that you can learn as much as possible from it.

Open your hearts as fully as possible and allow the experience, asking "what is there to learn here, and how is that best achieved?" Make that question a constant presence in daily living, so that it is always there just below the level of consciousness from which human life is lived and experienced.

Doing this, and regularly reminding yourselves to do it, will allow you to make great strides in increasing your mindfulness, until you find that, quite effortlessly, you are doing nothing unthinkingly; everything you do is done from your heart center, and very consciously.

This does not mean that your responses will be slow and labored; indeed quite the reverse, because by becoming more mindful, more aware, the distractions that previously influenced your reactions will just fall away, allowing your responses to be swift and appropriate, as your clarity of thought and situational awareness truly come into focus.

This, of course, will result in a deepening sense of peace and stability for you, as your inner knowing and intuition move nearer to the surface of your consciousness, and your life flows more and more smoothly as you actively, consciously, and most willingly follow the path that you have chosen.

In this state of increased peace and stability you will find it easier to understand and accept others with compassion, and this enables you to send them the energies of healing and love that are most appropriate.

This does not mean that you will ponder and then decide to send certain energies (that would be a judgmental approach!). It means that because of your love and acceptance of others, of humanity, of the Creator, that the appropriate energies for any situation will flow spontaneously from you under the direction and guidance of the divine One. You will be a true and undamaged channel through which divine energies, divinely directed, can and will flow. You will be allowing yourself, at the deepest and most spiritual level of your being, to be once more One with the divine Source.

So do your regular daily meditation. It is an absolutely essential part of the Creator's plan, and it is therefore absolutely essential that you do it. In time, all will meditate daily, joyfully, and with a great sense of peace and unity. Intend it and make it happen.

Ɵ   Ɵ   Ɵ

43   It is easy now for anyone to become aware of the awakening of humanity

Humanity's path of spiritual growth and development is truly turning into a multilane highway, as more and more of you begin to awaken from the illusory dream state in which the majority of you have been living for so long.

A major breakthrough was made quite a while ago — 40 to 50 years, as you experience time — which enabled the awakening process (which is always available to anyone, but taken up by very few) to start spreading at a steadily increasing rate through all of humanity's races, religions, and cultures.

It is very easy now for anyone to see and become aware of this, as more and more of you meet regularly, in groups of differing sizes, with the intent to become aware of, listen to, and respond purposefully and effectively to the divine guidance that each of you has available to you in every moment.

It brings great joy to those in other realms, as well as to your own human society, to see this awakening of awareness to the reality that there is a divine, creative Intelligence that loves, cherishes, and supports you in every moment.

As this realization dawns on people, it brings a surge of hope and relief, initially with the sense that "Maybe I am acceptable to and loved by the Creator." Once that thought establishes itself, it becomes apparent that this is indeed so, and that it is not possible that even one of you could *not* be loved unconditionally and eternally by God, because each of you is a perfect creation and therefore an expression of infinite, divine Love.

Many of you are now coming into blossom, like perfect flowers in a perfect divine garden, where none will ever fade and die. As more and more of you burst into bloom, the garden becomes increasingly beautiful, as always divinely intended. Each individual intent adds ever more beauty and wonder to this amazing garden of divine enchantment and bliss.

When you relax into the divine Presence as you pray, meditate, or just experience silence and peace, the divine creation that each one of you is shimmers, sparkles, and shines with an incredible variety of brilliant colors and hues that is truly magnificent to behold. God's Creation is absolutely wondrous to see and experience, and you are all awakening into the divine Reality that is All That Is, and vociferously claiming your divine heritage with delight, excitement, and overwhelming joy. Welcome Home!

ϴ   ϴ   ϴ

44   Peace and security are found within

A life on Earth as a human is an invaluable and much sought-after experience by those in the spiritual realms. It enables an entity to experience growth directly from chaos, which is the starting point of all creation and therefore filled with infinite potential. It allows opportunity and purpose, and perfect divine balance — to which all aspire — to occur.

In the spiritual realms, all is seen, all is known; and divine harmony always develops from the initial chaos.

As a human, the awareness, knowledge, and certainty of this is cloaked in the shadow of amnesia which an entity knowingly chooses to enter by becoming human. Within every human, at the deepest level of her existence, this knowledge is buried, but it cannot, and indeed is not meant to be, totally contained, and it seeps constantly and gently into awareness.

Frequently this seepage is misunderstood, misidentified, and discarded because it seems that the environment in which humanity appears to have its existence could in no way support the enlightenment, the magnificence of possibilities, and the divine truths and wonders at which these intimations hint.

Surrounded by the incredibly distorted unreality that humanity has created for itself over many, many lifetimes, it seems that truth, honesty, and enlightened communication are naive and unworkable modes of behavior, and the physical destruction of those who attempt it seems to prove time and again that humans cannot live harmoniously together, and in fact those who cheat and dissemble always win . . . or so it would appear.

But the winners expend enormous amounts of energy protecting their winnings and in attempting to win more, as they never seem to feel that they have enough. However, as they grow older, the energy required for this way of living becomes increasingly difficult to sustain, and they narrow their focus of awareness until it becomes a desperate and fear-driven defense of an untenable position that drives them to ever-deeper levels of bitterness and distrust, which is of course a mirror image of the untrustworthy way in which they have been living their lives. In short, betrayal begets betrayal.

On the other hand, those who genuinely live loving and caring lives, and who mostly do not focus on amassing material fortunes, enjoy a peace of mind and serenity that is health-giving and inspiring to themselves, and uplifting and encouraging to those with whom they interact. This is what the "winners" attempt to purchase — but of course it cannot be bought.

Peace and security are found within, and are nurtured and brought brilliantly to fruition by a life style that allows them free expression. Life can then become an inspiring art form, which can be learned and understood by experiencing life as a human.

But a human is also open to all the seductions of the environment in which he chooses to experience his existence. They are often so noisy and apparently glamorous that the messages and guidance from deep within the self are completely drowned out by the cacophony of distractions in the entity's human surroundings.

And so, teacher after teacher has emphasized time and again the need for solitude, the need to go within and listen to the heart, the soul, the spirit, the divine guidance to which everyone has constant access, and which so very many refuse to acknowledge in their unending external quest for what in fact resides within.

You have so many phrases in your many human languages to describe this condition: "The grass is always greener on the other side" being the basic one in western cultures, meaning that somewhere else is always better than here. And this is a fundamental refusal to see how wonderful and perfect your situation is right now (in the context of the life path you planned). Of course it is . . . . You planned your life very carefully, choosing in advance a plethora of experiences and opportunities to provide you with the many lessons that you decided you wanted to learn during this particular incarnation.

You also arranged for a team of guides to be constantly available to help you and show you the way in every moment. You have only to call on them with your needs and requests, and they will respond instantly. But you have to open your mind and your heart to hear what they say. If you are convinced that the only solution to your problem is an ego-oriented or material one, such as more money, more power, or more freedom, then you are energetically blocking the true solutions, the spiritual solutions — of which there are many — that you provided in your life plan before you incarnated, and of which your guides, in response to your call for help, are trying to remind you.

When you seek help from the spiritual realms, it is essential that you relax and open your heart to your intuitive guidance, and that you completely release any preconceived solutions you may have considered, so that the abundant joyful opportunities that those in the spiritual realms can assist you to access can come into your awareness. You need to also release completely any desire to judge, blame, or condemn yourself or others for the predicament for which you are seeking guidance, and to prepare yourself for a solution that in three-dimensional terms may appear to come from a most unexpected quarter.

Limiting the area from which you are willing to accept guidance and solutions severely restricts your ability to resolve your difficulties, and may well prevent you from recognizing a solution that makes spiritual winners out of all involved, thereby missing the joyful satisfaction that a truly creative and cooperative venture can provide.

45   God does not judge

When you live on Earth as humans, your life supplies you with many varied experiences to enable you to learn the numerous lessons that are required in order for you to develop your full potential. Each lesson is complete in itself, but also builds on the ones that have gone before it and prepares the way for the ones that are to follow. The rapidity with which you learn each lesson and the time interval between each one is very much up to you.

Often, when life seems to become too intense, a person will take a break and cut back on his growing awareness of his reason for existence. This is possibly because he feels that he has not used his Heaven-sent opportunities to the best of his abilities, or because of an apparent failure by him to behave in the way that he imagines God expects, and he feels unworthy to know God or ask for His help.

If he finds himself in this situation, it is very difficult for him to move forward. This is why it is so important not to judge. Judgment nearly always involves blame and a sense of shame, placing a cloak of unworthiness on the one so judged — including oneself.

God does not judge. He loves and encourages, and He wants His children to do likewise. All of you have "sinned!" It is part of living as humans, and the lesson that sin teaches is that forgiveness and acceptance are guaranteed! Sin is merely an error that can and will be corrected.

Like everything else in life, it is a lesson, and when the lesson is learned you move on, and sin is no longer an issue. Yes, of course mistakes and errors will still be made, but they are not sins. They may be due to inattention, inadequate preparation, or insufficient knowledge; whereas sin is a choice consciously made — even if not admitted — to behave improperly.

As all have sinned, it is quite inappropriate to judge another; judgment implies that the judge is superior to, and more righteous than, the one being judged. Change the action that is being judged, and the roles of the judge and the one being judged may well be reversed!

When errors are made, or sins are committed, the creative response is communication and cooperation to resolve the situation. No one is above criticism, and engaging in criticism without a tremendous amount of careful preparation and discussion is normally very destructive.

Accept your humanity and the multitude of learning opportunities that it provides, and help one another lovingly and wisely to obtain the maximum benefit from it by communicating and working together. If you do this you will change the world; and all that now causes pain, fear, anger, distrust, and general disharmony will just dissolve in that wondrous and almighty solvent : Love!

Ɵ   Ɵ   Ɵ

46   The opportunities for humanity to work with power are many and varied

There is so much to tell you about God's divine plan for Planet Earth and humanity, that many, many lifetimes would be necessary if I were to give you more than a brief glimpse of what He has in store for you. Many of His more wondrous intentions would be totally beyond your ability to comprehend at all in your present state of spiritual development. But as you progress along your path of spiritual growth, ever more wonderful vistas will open up before you for your delight and amazement.

God designed all sentient beings for continuous spiritual development. Getting started on that path is difficult because much is demanded of you, and yet every human has the potential for infinite spiritual growth, and every single one will achieve it.

However, there tends to be much stumbling and back-sliding in the early stages, which can be very unsettling and discouraging. But enormous quantities of precisely designed assistance are available to each one who asks for it. And asking is essential. Assistance may not be imposed because you have free will, which is itself a most wonderful gift.

So during your regular prayer/meditation/relaxation periods ask intensely, powerfully, insistently for help and guidance, and you will receive it in abundance. And ask for the grace to accept it and understand it.

The environment in which you have chosen to undergo human life has many seductive and intriguing experiences and opportunities to offer you. And while they are an essential part of that environment to assist you in your spiritual growth, they can also seriously distract you from your life's purpose.

Earth provides you with an environment in which you can practice your creative skills and learn to use them wisely and well. But to create, you need power, and that power is incredibly seductive, especially if you are moving on from an experience of powerlessness. It can seduce you into using it just because you can.

It is essential for you to learn and fully understand the divine Intent that allows power to be available to you. God always uses power for the benefit of all of His creation. There are no compromises here. It is always used for good and does not cause damage or disharmony anywhere. If it caused good in one place and harm somewhere else, it would not be harmonious, loving, and respectful of all, and therefore would not be divine.

The opportunities for humanity to work with power are many and varied in your earthly environment, but they are restricted to that environment to ensure that any damage caused by misuse affects only those who have chosen to experience earthly existence.

The apparent chaos, mayhem, and destruction that occurs in your environment due to the misuse of power is localized and contained by divine Intent. It is a very potent learning experience for all humans and leads to an understanding of the immense responsibility and mindfulness required in its use — always.

What is happening on Planet Earth today is a truly fast-track learning-curve for all about the disastrous consequences of misused or abusively used power. It is very intense and will be quite short-lived.

The need for harmonious agreement prior to taking powerful action is becoming increasingly apparent as the fallout from recent, self-serving human activities becomes clear for all to see. It demonstrates the insanity of acting powerfully without first ensuring that every result of that action is foreseen and understood.

As your general level of consciousness grows, and also your awareness that you are always responsible for your actions, so the abuse of power on Earth will decrease rapidly. It will cease altogether far sooner than you can imagine, as more and more of you spend time praying for and intending to receive divine assistance to heal the planet and heal humanity.

47 . Every human is being nudged into wakefulness

A tremendous amount of rapid progress is being made with regard to the general awakening of humanity. Every human is being nudged into wakefulness, although some do go back to sleep and require further nudges.

The divine plan for humanity is proceeding exactly as divinely intended, and will always continue to do so. Those who are awake and those who are awakening are creating enormous waves of spiritual energy, which greatly assist in raising the consciousness and awareness levels of all of humanity.

So continue to do what you are doing, and maintain a positive attitude! Your attitude is yours to shape and adjust.

You know deep within yourselves that the divine plan is perfectly wonderful and perfectly on schedule. Allow that knowledge into your conscious awareness at every moment — and be in joy; that is what you are here to do. Let go of your misperceptions, which focus your attention on the negative and on the non-spiritual, because that gives them energy and thus drains you.

You are powerful beings — divinely guided. Allow the divine energy to flow through you freely. . . because it is one of your reasons for being here. It will delight you, and strengthen and empower others. Stop seeing yourselves as inadequate, because that is a misperception which you keep embracing. Let it go!

God created you perfect — allow yourselves to be that. . . . That is all you have to do: allow and accept. Be courageously yourselves, and delight in the experience. Apart from the joy it brings you, it also assists and strengthens the abilities that others have to do likewise. It is your human destiny — and it is happening right now. You cannot be shamed, because you are divine creations, perfectly crafted — and you know it. Just let yourselves be aware of it, and bring this knowledge to the attention and awareness of others, so that they too can awaken to the truth and wonder of their own divine perfection.

This is how all will come to full consciousness. . . by the raising of awareness that all are divine creations about to burst into bloom. It is a state that will bring ecstasy and delight in existence into the conscious awareness of every human.

Those who wish may of course refuse it and draw the blinds, but the vast majority of humanity — beautiful and perfect beings that you are — will embrace it with a happiness and joy so deep and intense that it cannot even be hinted at in words. And the experience, when you accept it into your wonderful loving hearts will be for always, eternal, continuously present, endless.

It is God's desire and intent for you — indeed, your divine inheritance — and it is utterly breathtaking in its scope and immensity. You exist in an atmosphere of the most intense, divine, unconditional Love. So stop holding your breath, just breathe deeply. . . and truly come alive.

Θ   Θ   Θ

48   The changes will astound even those of you who have been most actively preparing for this time

As you know, many, many changes are occurring on Earth at this point in its evolution. Much seems violent and inappropriate, but it involves a much-needed release of long-held and deeply embedded, untenable beliefs and perceptions whose influence is finished and whose time is past. The release is indeed causing much short term pain, which will quickly dissolve as the new era of peace, harmony, and prosperity for all comes flooding in on the tidal wave of divine Love that is about to engulf the planet.

The changes in the environment and in your life styles that are about to occur are truly remarkable, and will astound and amaze you all, even those of you who have been most actively preparing for this time.

Fear and distrust will fade away as you realize that there is no need for them. All will find that they are respected and accepted wherever they go — just for themselves, for who they are. No one will any longer feel it necessary to attempt to justify their existence. This has always been the case, but now all will know this, deep within the peace and harmony of their own beingness.

The ways of God are truly amazing, and the way in which the divine plan unfolds — perfectly — always — is an unimaginable joy to behold.

Those of you who have been holding the vision on Earth of divine abundance, peace, harmony, and prosperity for all of humanity have had your faith sorely tested, as you have worked basically in the dark about what is unfolding — frequently, and for many Earth lifetimes — as you have struggled to bring forth the Light while effectively disconnected from the main power grid. For that is how life is experienced on Earth at present, and yet you have persisted and returned many times to the Earth experience of pain and frustration, because deep within yourselves you have always known what you were doing, what you were preparing for, and that a totally wondrous and successful outcome was inevitable.

That moment is indeed at hand. So relax, meditate, pray, and open your hearts to receive, accept, and enjoy the abundant divine outpourings which have long been prepared for you, and which are your rightful heritage.

All is coming rapidly and forcefully together to create on Earth the divine, heavenly environment that was planned for this glorious planet and its wonderful, divinely guided inhabitants, before time, as you experience it, existed. Every single human's existence and participation has been absolutely essential to the divine creative plan for Planet Earth. Every one of you has contributed in her or his own unique and irreplaceable way, and you will continue to contribute eternally in ever-increasing joy and bliss.

God, the divine Creator, loves each one of you with an infinite tenderness, and there is nothing you can do about it. So open your hearts and accept His infinite Love and acceptance which is offered to you now, and forever.

ϴ   ϴ   ϴ

49   Holding the intent for global peace has great power

The world as portrayed by your news media does indeed seem an alarming place, and humanity does have a penchant for focusing on what is unpleasant and negative.

Attention does need to be directed at those aspects but not to the extent that the media does, and not to the extent of ignoring what is good, happy, and positive, of which there is indeed much. An amazing amount is being done worldwide to relieve poverty and the misery of those living in poverty. But on the whole these successes are not trumpeted in the media. Yet they are increasing in number and frequency as more and more people respond to God's divine call to love your neighbor as yourselves.

The tide on that front has truly turned, and Love — an energy of unimaginable power and strength — is flowing onto the planet in increasing abundance, and changing the precepts upon which people everywhere base their philosophy of life.

All are becoming aware of the urgent need for cooperation, and for the peace, harmony, and universal prosperity to which it leads. Those of you who think that all you are doing is praying, meditating, and hoping are doing far, far more on other levels, so your lack of physical participation in waking life is not a valid indication of your overall involvement. Holding the intent for global peace and prosperity in every moment of your lives has great power and is a most important part of the divine plan. You do not need to be conscious of the intent in every moment, because by holding it you make it happen, as you live the intent in your daily lives.

If you feel attracted to becoming more involved on the physical level, then do so. But follow your heart, your gut feelings, your inner guidance. And know that all manner of things will be well.

Θ   Θ   Θ

50   And you truly will begin to see the Divine in everyone

Your life is a challenge — a challenge that you created for yourselves before you incarnated as humans for your present life experiences. The challenge is to grow and develop spiritually so that your God-given talents may be used to the full in an environment that desperately needs them.

If you arrived with those talents already fully developed, you would stand out as being very different from other members of human society, and therefore anything you achieved would be seen as something special, something only achievable by the very few, as opposed to something that any human can achieve if they were prepared to put in the time and the effort.

All humans are divine, because each one of them is an individual and unique part of the divine creation. As such, each one of you has immense power available to you if you will but seek it out and intend to have it.

The whole purpose is to create Heaven wherever you are by truly being your unique self. The vast majority of humans buy into the cultural environment into which they are born, with all its rules, regulations, judgments, punishments, and, very infrequently, rewards.

All around you, you see and experience injustice, and you make the assessment that life is unfair, and that more rules, regulations, and punishments must be introduced in attempts to make it fair. You buy into the belief that humans are treacherous, untrustworthy beings, and you find this regularly demonstrated by the way people treat, and cheat on, each other. You conclude that the only way to get your own fair share is to behave likewise. You remonstrate with others about their dishonesty and lack of integrity, and justify your own as being necessary for survival. You believe that when the world becomes a fairer place, you will then also behave fairly.

This attitude feeds beautifully on itself; no one can be found who is trustworthy, as all wait for others to change or attempt to force others to comply with their own narrow views of what is right and wrong. This insane form of behavior has bedeviled humanity for many thousands of years. Crime, punishment, war, persecution, intolerance, and desire for vengeance have flourished in all your cultures throughout history. What has been achieved but more of the same? You will not learn.

If you would fully use your God-given talents, you would see that each one of you truly is unique and therefore only capable of changing himself.

You knew that before you incarnated; and you planned to live with honesty, integrity, and compassion as a human. However, the energies of distrust and betrayal that have grown out of humanity's violent behavior over very many generations is pervasive — and indeed seductive! — making it very difficult for you to remember and act on the intentions you made before incarnating.

You can only change yourself. Release your fear and your anger, and treat everyone with love and compassion. To do this you must first fully accept and fully forgive yourself. Look at the aspects of yourself that you have judged unsatisfactory, unacceptable, or shameful. Look hard at them and realize that they are aspects of yourself that have been badly hurt and damaged, and that they need love and healing, not condemnation.

Realize that others are similarly hurt, and learn to be gentle with one another. If your body is physically damaged, you have to treat the hurt part gently until it is healed, and you have to continue to do so after healing has occurred so that it can regain its strength.

Your spirit gets hurt by psychic and emotional damage, which you frequently do not acknowledge, so the pain is buried out of sight and out of mind, where it festers and affects your attitude to life and to others. It may develop into physical disease or damage — your stomach truly does keep count. So, bearing in mind constantly that all humans are damaged and hurting to a greater or lesser extent, treat everyone with respect, love, and compassion.

Listen to and hear and understand the needs of others (their true needs, not their attempts to manipulate people), and respond appropriately with love, wisdom, and compassion, thereby assisting them to satisfy those needs. By allowing them to talk, and by listening to them quietly and compassionately, you will help them to hear and understand themselves, and so learn what it is they truly desire from life.

Life is a learning experience of incalculable value. Allow yourselves to learn as you live fully in every moment. Open your awareness. . . see what is going on, on every level — physical, emotional, psychic, and spiritual. You do have the sensors to tune in and understand.

When you do this and start to experience this understanding of people, you will be amazed at the love and compassion that will fill your hearts. And you will truly begin to see the Divine in everyone.

51   Accidents are the body's attempts to get your attention

As you live day by day, moment by moment, the divine energy that the Creator pours forth continuously and abundantly permeates your entire being — if you will allow it — leading you forward along your chosen path in peace and harmony with all of creation.

When you construct blockages or dams that restrict the flow of energy, problems occur in direct response and proportion to the barriers you choose to erect. The problems are a perfectly natural reaction to these barriers, and serve to bring to your attention the fact that your life is out of balance and that you need to do something to correct it.

If you choose to ignore the signals you are receiving, the imbalance will increase in severity until — if you choose to remain in ignorance — it causes physical damage to your body, which may occur as an illness or as an accident. All physical bodily damage is a result of ignoring the warning signals that you have been receiving.

Regular relaxation and meditation are essential to your physical well-being. Everyone needs time alone every day to listen to their body telling them of its needs. Often the information comes through very quietly and subtly, which is why you need to quieten your mind by meditating, as this enables you to become aware of these subtle signals.

An unquiet mind prevents awareness and personal wisdom from coming into your consciousness. Without this inner knowing and wisdom that God makes constantly available to you, your life becomes an incomprehensible tangle, like a heap of cold congealed spaghetti! Untangling it, without taking time out to be alone, is impossible; and yet the tendency is to become noisier and busier the more tangled it becomes.

If the tangling becomes severe, illnesses or accidents often occur as the body desperately attempts to get your attention. And sometimes the shock this causes does lead the person to self-reflection and a reevaluation of their life style. If it does not, then further illnesses or accidents are likely to occur; the body does not give up until it is lifeless! Be aware and listen to it. It always has something of importance to tell you.

Θ Θ Θ

52 An amazing increase in spiritual awareness is occurring all over the planet

Living is humanity's task. And in order to live well, awareness of the unbreakable connection to our Creator is essential. The seeds of this knowledge are buried deep in the heart center of every human. Prayer, meditation, day dreaming, and relaxed inactivity nourish those seeds and encourage their growth. All will nourish the seeds within, and the vast and continuous downpour of divine graces and blessings onto Planet Earth at this time assures healthy growth when the individual allows herself to become aware and seeks spiritual knowledge and guidance.

It is wonderful to see the amazing increase in spiritual awareness that is occurring all over the planet and the resulting, very large increase in the numbers of you praying and meditating daily. The strength of your desire and intent for the implementation of the divine Golden Age is a joy to see. Humanity is truly moving forward towards that point — the moment when it will be ushered in — with increasing intensity and desire.

The energies of love, wisdom, acceptance, and healing that humanity is creating in every moment — with immensely powerful assistance from the divine realms — are more powerful and effective than at any other time on Planet Earth.

It is, of course, all part of the divine plan, but to observe it in operation in every moment is quite wonderful. So many of you are becoming aware of the power that you can access to anchor, strengthen, and expand these creative energies; and in your awareness lies the key, the knowledge, and the ability to bring yourselves into the state of full consciousness that has always been the divine Intent for you.

The moment in which you will achieve this state is approaching very rapidly. So continue your regular periods of prayer and meditation, and increase their frequency so that you are effectively praying and meditating in every moment as a constant background to all your activities. In this way you add powerfully and constantly to the divine energies and Intent, preparing yourselves and making yourselves ready to accept the divine gift of full consciousness, so that you can move easily and joyfully into that heavenly state, as God has always willed and intended.

Truly humanity is now very close to achieving its divine destiny. God loves you all with a passion and intensity that, in your terms, is quite mind-blowing. And when you move into the state of full consciousness, as you surely and inevitably will, the joy of that experience will be truly awesome for you.

Every one of you passionately desires to be loved, and so very many of you have spent lifetimes searching for the partner, the companion, the other who will love you as you want to be loved. But each of you has always been loved far more intensely and passionately than, as humans, you can possibly imagine.

And you continue to be so loved, eternally; it is just that in your human state, it is not possible to experience that intensity of love because it would literally burn you up.

However, when you move into full consciousness, as you surely will, you will once again experience the total bliss of being divinely loved, and you will remember and experience the memory that you always have been loved divinely and passionately by God. Your joy and delight will know no limits because there are no limits to God's Love for each one of you.

Ɵ   Ɵ   Ɵ

53   Life has many ways to attract your attention

Life has many ways of attracting your attention and asking you what it is all about. It has a purpose — a very important purpose — that deep within yourselves you know. But you are easily distracted and caught up in the seduction of the physical world, and so life needs to attract your attention to bring you back to consider the reason for your existence, which is to learn to know God.

His Love for you is infinite — unimaginable in human terms — and as you learn to know Him your love for Him will grow until it overwhelms you with joy. Learning to know Him is very easy, because He is your Teacher, and as such He is of course perfect, and His lessons are easy. You have only to ask and allow, and then you will learn.

When you relax into a meditative state, and intend and allow His Love to envelop and suffuse you, it does. And then, as you go about your day, His grace and energy continue to flow through you, strengthening and empowering you. This will bring you increasing peace and contentment and assist you in bringing harmony, understanding, compassion, and cooperation to every situation in which you find yourselves. This is why I keep reminding you to take time out frequently during the day to renew your intent to allow God's Love to envelop and flow through you.

When you find yourselves feeling upset, anxious, angry, irritated, or fearful, it is a call to remind you to take time out in that moment to renew your intent. When you do so, it will remind you that you are immersing yourselves in the divine light of the Creator's Love, and the sense or feeling of being upset will dissolve and dissipate into that vast ocean of Love of which you are an essential part.

All truly are one; separation is an illusion with which you are working in order to return to the absolute wonder of knowing and experiencing the knowledge that you are eternally part — an absolutely essential and irreplaceable part — of the Creator.

To know that and to experience it is to fill yourselves with overwhelming joy, completely and utterly secure in your inseparability from God for even a moment. To be separate from Him would be to cease to exist, and that is impossible because you are part of that-which-cannot-be-divided, cannot be broken up or separated into pieces. You are permanently in the divine Presence in every moment of your existence. If you are unaware of this — and the vast majority of humanity is unaware — it is because you have chosen to be.

That lack of awareness causes you intense pain, fear, anger, and confusion. So cease your unawareness; open your hearts and invite God to fill them with the light of His Love, and allow Him to do so. That is all it takes to bring you back to a preliminary state of peace and contentment, as you continue your progress towards full consciousness. So do it now.

Ɵ   Ɵ   Ɵ

54   Love strengthens you enormously — physically and spiritually

Much is happening on your world at present that is not reported in the mass media. Vast amounts of divine energy and assistance are raining down on your planet, and you need only hold the intent and desire to receive it, and you will — abundantly. It is very powerful and, when absorbed by you, strengthens you enormously — physically and spiritually. It enables you to intensify your love for all of humanity and makes it much easier for you to practice unconditional love, which is the purest form of love with which you can work in your physical state as humans.

Love, as you are well aware, is the energy that drives creation and, consequently, is intensely powerful. It has to be very much stepped down and reduced in power from the equivalent of an all-encompassing ocean storm to the energy of a small spring in your backyard to enable humanity to work with it at all. When you move into full consciousness and begin to experience and use Love as you are meant to, you will be filled with awe and wonder at the infinite opportunities that it provides.

It is Love that is enabling humanity to make such rapid spiritual progress at this time, as it erodes and washes away the granite-like layers of protection in which fear, hate, and pain have encased your human hearts. As more and more of you awaken to the need for a spiritual direction in your lives and start to understand the need to behave respectfully and lovingly to all with whom you interact, and then put that understanding into practice, you become aware of an increasing sense of peace and satisfaction in your lives.

The love force is truly sweeping across the planet and bringing great changes in the way people respond to one another. And you are all beginning to notice it. The media continues to focus on the mistrust, hate, and fear that continues to fester in various places on Earth, and fails to see, or chooses to ignore, the love that is dissolving those energies everywhere else on the planet.

Very soon the love force will be felt and make its presence very apparent in those remaining war zones and areas where human confrontation and disagreement continue to flourish. They too will then be inundated by the divine energy of Love that is rolling in everywhere to enable and bring into effect humanity's return to full consciousness.

So relax, meditate, and allow the divine energies to suffuse and empower you, as they most surely will, if that is your intent and your desire.

55   Make a daily intent to accept yourself — just as you are

As you start to grow and develop spiritually, many issues float to the surface of your awareness with which you need to deal. It is an essential part of the awakening process, and it can be very uncomfortable, unsettling, and even painful. But the issues do have to be addressed to enable your spiritual growth to continue.

When you find yourselves in this situation— as all of you will as you awaken into a wider awareness of the human life experience — it is of enormous help to make a daily intent to forgive and accept yourselves — just as you are — and to forgive and accept all others with whom you interact. Then ask for guidance and help from the spiritual realms to put that intent into practice. This is the first step in solving the difficulties and problems with which these issues present you, and in releasing the emotional patterning that caused them.

The more positively and frequently you renew this intent, the more swiftly will these issues be dealt with and released. Each release or letting-go brings more peace and harmony into your lives and makes the remaining issues easier to release.

As you become more peaceful you will also become more content, your lives will become more balanced, and you will notice that your interactions with others will flow far more smoothly. Others will also notice the change and will feel the peace and harmony of the energies that are extending from you, and they will tend to respond in a similar manner.

This is basically a most wonderful self-healing process that everyone can avail of, if they so intend, and it has a very positive and powerful knock-on effect. Those who encounter its energy field — and they will when they interact with anyone who is working through this process — will themselves be prompted to awaken and look within. These promptings can be very delicate and subtle, or very intense and powerful attention-grabbers, depending on the needs and deep inner intentions of the individuals concerned. But all who come into contact with one of these energy fields will most certainly be affected by it. How they choose to respond is always entirely up to them.

So when you get into this process, be aware that you do carry and share a very positive energy charge, which is basically unconditional love. Intend that it surround and envelop you and that those who come into contact with you receive precisely what is appropriate for them in that moment. Do not attempt to direct it, as it has its own divine guidance. Just be content to have it flow through you and around you, and give thanks for it to your loving Father who so perfectly provides you with everything you need.

Ɵ   Ɵ   Ɵ

56   The enormous damage to Mother Earth is in fact a cleansing and rebirthing exercise

These times are indeed stressful for you, your families, and for humanity in general. As the end times for human existence (as humanity has presently come to understand and experience it) draws to a close, there will indeed be considerable alarm and confusion until people begin to understand what is occurring on their massively hurt and damaged planet.

At first it will seem that the damage is increasing exponentially, until it becomes apparent that the new and enormous damage is in fact a cleansing and rebirthing exercise to restore

Earth to her former glory, in which she and all the life forms she supports cooperate in a mutually harmonious, peaceful, and beautiful existence, where the needs of all are supremely well-balanced and abundantly provided for.

Everything is now moving into high gear to encourage and expedite the move into the new Golden Age of peace, love, and wisdom which will heal, cure, and eradicate all the physical and psychic pain and damage that have built up over eons of time to the cumulatively disastrous levels seen and experienced today on this beautiful planet. All who wish it will be healed and rejuvenated very quickly once the planetary changes are complete.

To express the wish for healing and to move into the new age, it is only necessary to hold the intent to do so through meditation, prayer, or ritual and through the honest opening of your hearts in loving acceptance of what is happening. It truly is very simple. . . . Just relax into this new, all-enveloping reality that is coming into being, and go with the flow. Your intent, and the infinitely loving divine Intent of the Creator will take care of the details quickly and easily. Your paradise has been prepared and awaits you. Enter joyfully, knowing that you are returning to your rightful Home.

Ɵ Ɵ Ɵ

57 Attempting to control your lives creates a tremendous drag on your progress

As time passes, your sense of self, who you are, becomes more consistent and centered, because your meditation and relaxation practice will allow your lives to flow naturally, instead of you trying to control its flow.

You chose a path to follow, and the junctions and turning-points are all clearly marked. All that you have to do is allow yourselves to make the appropriate turns as they occur. If you will allow it, your inner knowing, your intuition, will not fail you or let you down. You will move easily through life and experience it as a constant flow that carries you with it. Of course there will be rough patches and obstructions, but the natural flowing of your lives will cope with them very easily — if you will allow it.

When you attempt to control and direct the flow of your lives in a materialistic manner — looking for security in money, position, property, etc. — it may or may not work; you see both successful and unsuccessful people out there. But in spiritual terms (and you are here to grow and develop spiritually), it creates a tremendous drag on your progress, and can stall it completely for an entire lifetime.

This is by no means a disaster, because eventually you will progress as planned. But it does mean that you will become confused and discouraged as your sense of meaning or purpose is at first distorted and then lost altogether. Witness so many old people who are unhappy with their lives and circumstances, and are terrified of death, yet remain unwilling to face up to the fact that it is going to happen to them. They fill their remaining years with trivial distractions as they try to avoid being aware of the continual wake-up call they are receiving which asks them "What is it all about?"

They are afraid to think about it because they fear that they will discover that they have missed their life's purpose and wasted their lives. Of course they have not wasted their lives (a life cannot be wasted), but they have allowed fear to rule it, and have closed their minds in a futile attempt to hide from this fact.

Fear is supposed to wake you up and get your attention. But

you yourselves fill your lives with imagined and unnecessary fears that create an overload with which you cannot possibly cope. And so the fuse blows, and you shut down and distract yourselves with trivia.

It is as though you had drifted into a stagnant backwater and decided to stay there as the river of life flows by, because you prefer scrambling about in the mud, pretending to yourselves that you are lost and can do nothing about it.

And of course you are perfectly free to play that game for as long as you wish. . . until you finally decide to realize that it is you who have trapped and made victims of yourselves. No one else, not even God made you do it!

And then you move on. You can always move on. . . at any time. The traps are all of your own making. They are mirages that exist only in your imagination.

θ   θ   θ

58   Welcome your fallow periods

When your life flows easily for you it is good to recall times when you were stressed out or under a lot of pressure, so that you may implant firmly in your experience bank the knowledge that difficult times will and do pass.

Time always passes, although the speed at which you experience it passing varies — but you are always moving on. Moving and learning go together; both are continually happening in your life, but it is up to you — your choice — how you experience them. If you are open of heart and mind, much growth takes place. And if not, it feels as though you are achieving very little.

This is not necessarily so, because later on, as you reflect back,

107

you may well see much that was not apparent to you in the moment. On the other hand what you actually learned may remain unknown, hidden from you in this lifetime. However, you have learnt it, and it is stored deep within you.

So be aware that life always has tremendous meaning and vitality, even if it is not apparent to you.

Periods when it seems (to others as well!) that you are stagnating, or apparently lost and wandering aimlessly, are in facts periods when much is going on deep within you. At such times the normal distraction of human interests is blocked so that you remain quiet and accessible on deeper levels.

It does feel uncomfortable, but much is going on; so do not discount it or rail against it. Just welcome your fallow periods, knowing that they are times of very necessary preparation for your next stages of growth.

Θ Θ Θ

59 Humanity just does not get it

Humanity just does not get it! God's Love is infinite and unconditional, and is offered to all. Only acceptance of it is required. There is no Divine Judgment; humanity has more than enough of its own! You are here to learn to live in peace, harmony, and unconditional love with each other and with your gloriously beautiful planet. If you would stop judging one another and begin listening to each others' needs and desires, and then adjust your own requirements so that they do not impinge on the requirements of others, your lives would flow much more smoothly.

One of your biggest problems is incredibly low individual self-esteem, which you try to cure by joining organizations such as

108

clubs, teams, gangs, religious and business communities — the list is endless. You then spend your time judging the groups to which you do not belong as inferior, wrong, misinformed, misled, a waste of time, damaging, etc. Then you either try to impose your beliefs on them or destroy them. And the organization to which you belong encourages and exaggerates your low sense of self-esteem by its rules and the penalties it enforces for breaking them, to make sure that your dependency on it grows and deepens.

As humans grow from childhood to maturity, their cultural and ethnic imprints harden and stabilize, making it very difficult for them to alter their beliefs in any meaningful way. Small changes that appear to be logical developments resulting from wiser and more mature reflection on those beliefs do not change anything. They merely maintain the status quo by allowing small alterations as a sop to the next generation. And these changes, although often greeted with a great fanfare of trumpet blowing, are truly just the minor alterations one gets from tinkering ineffectually with the system.

The longer you belong to an organization, the more difficult it becomes to leave, as your feeling of dependency on it only strengthens with the passage of time.

Why do you think so many people die quite soon after retirement? It is because they have to all intents been banished by the organization on which they have come to depend totally. It is very similar to a native tribe that withdraws approval and recognition from one of its members for some crime against the tribe. This action is basically a death sentence, and within a very short time the person so ostracized will die.

So, work on building a strong sense of personal self-esteem. God created every one of you out of infinite unconditional Love, and you are thus entitled to value yourself very highly indeed — as does your Creator.

Be very sure to encourage and assist the growth of self-esteem in your children, and in fact in everyone with whom you interact. The human condition has children born in total dependency, but they are also programmed to move steadily into independence as they grow and develop; and it is a very heavy responsibility that a parent has to provide a safe environment in which the growing child can experiment and play with independence until that becomes its natural state.

Those who are truly independent are always respecters of the rights and dignity of others and are therefore best able to cooperate and share in peace and harmony. You are all responsible for the world in which you live, because you are continuously creating it as you believe it to be. If you do not like your beliefs, then change them. When you meditate ask for guidance and help to change them, and for help to become fully aware of your intuition, your gut feelings, which are provided to enable you to grow, develop, and blossom into the fullness of humanity which is your entitlement and your goal.

A fully developed human is a most wonderful being, and you are all — every single one of you, no matter what your ethnic, cultural, or religious origins may be — programmed to become one. Allow it to happen to you. Open your hearts and accept your Father's unconditional Love for you, and grow and mature in the loving wisdom that He has provided for you.

You will be amazed, astounded, and delighted at the results if you truly invite Him into your hearts and accept His Presence there with you. You will know that you are totally loved, cherished, and of inestimable value to Him, because you are, and because He will make it known to you.

60   Make allowances for even the most unpleasant and unruly humans

Your time on Earth as humans provides great opportunities for you to further your spiritual development rapidly and effectively. Your apparent lack of connection to the higher realms of existence means that you act on faith, on intuition, on gut feelings. So what you do and intend does not have a guaranteed outcome; you hope things will turn out as you intend, and you work to enable that intent. Yet, quite frequently the unexpected happens.

However, you continue to live your lives, make plans, and work hard to bring them to fruition. You do not let your failures keep you from attempting to achieve results that you consider worthwhile or necessary. This persistence that you demonstrate during your short span on Earth is amazingly effective in encouraging, optimizing, and speeding up your spiritual growth. Life as a human is in fact a catalyst for spiritual growth that is not available to you in the higher-frequency realms of existence that you inhabit when you are not in human form.

When you move back to other realms after physical death, most of you are truly amazed at what an apparently humdrum and ordinary human existence has enabled you to achieve on these higher levels.

So be aware and know that what you are doing while you are a human is creating the most wonderful treasures for you to return to when your Earth life is completed. Even though it may seem impossible to you, the most violently unpleasant beings that exist in your environment as humans, creating apparent havoc and mayhem, also build up great treasures in the spiritual realms by their actions while on Earth. Remember that on Earth all is frequently not as it seems. So make allowances for even the most unpleasant and unruly humans. Send them love and compassion, and absolutely refrain from judging them.

When you return to the spiritual realms in glory, as you all most assuredly will, you will understand what has been going on on the Earth plane, and realize the magnificence and wonder of God's divine plan for you all. He loves His creation infinitely, in ways that are completely beyond your ability to understand, and He will never allow anything to interfere with your progress back to the treasure house of Oneness with Him.

Relax and meditate frequently and regularly every day during your lives and allow the help and guidance that you chose to have available to you in every moment to awaken you to your passion, your heart's desire, so that you may live the lives you planned for yourselves before you incarnated.

Every one of you made the most marvelous life plans for yourselves, and by relaxing and opening your hearts to your divinely inspired guidance you will enable yourselves to follow them effortlessly. You will know that you are following your path because you will feel contentment and satisfaction with your life, even when dealing with trials and tribulations. And deep within yourselves you will know that all is well and is going as planned; that you are indeed walking in the sight and in the light of God.

Θ Θ Θ

61   Every hope or expectation you have ever dreamed of will be infinitely surpassed

The moment for humanity's move into full consciousness is approaching rapidly, and much preparation is taking place to ensure that the celebrations to mark this transition to a wholly new way of experiencing life, existence, and God's infinite unconditional Love for each one of you, are absolutely magnificent in every way.

I have told you before of the utmost intensity of joy that you will soon experience permanently, when you move or expand into full consciousness, and I want to reconfirm for you that this is so. Your happiness and joy will know no limits, your satisfaction will be total, complete, way beyond your present ability to imagine in any meaningful way.

God's Love for you all is beyond imagination or conception in human terms, and very shortly you will experience it. . . constantly. . . eternally.

Your world leaders, who have been confused and misguided

for so long, are beginning to awaken, and this is leading to enormous changes of perception about the meaning of life on your glorious planet. Truly, great changes of a most momentous nature will occur very shortly that will astound and delight all of humanity. Your prayers, intentions, and meditative practices have had a most profound effect on your environment, and this is about to become apparent to all in the most glorious way.

Your sufferings, pains, fears, and depressions will be swept away as the divine Golden Age for Planet Earth — that has been planned and intended since before time, as you experience it, came to be — comes flooding brilliantly into the life that each one of you experiences.

It is individually tailored, designed, and arranged so that what each one of you experiences is divinely perfect for you. Your joy will be total as you meld with God, with each other, with all in the spiritual realms, in fact with All That Is, in a most magnificent union that wholly honors all of you.

It is impossible to give you even the slightest glimpse of the joy you are all about to experience permanently. Just know — as you truly do, deep within yourselves — that God's divine plan is infinitely loving and bountiful, and that every hope or expectation you have ever dreamed of will be infinitely surpassed as you return home to the glory that is yours.

Θ   Θ   Θ

62   Accept the flow of life

Life is truly full of delightful surprises. . . if you will only allow yourselves to open up and be aware.

To spend lots of time worrying anxiously about how others perceive you, about how you can control your relationships, about obtaining justice or revenge for damage done to you by others is a massive distraction from living. It prevents you from living in the moment and delighting in life, because all the time you are either recalling the past or waiting for the future. And life is now. . . this present moment. . . that you just missed!

As you practice awareness, during meditation, while listening to music, while washing the dishes, driving the car, taking a shower or going for a walk, you will find your awareness opening up and your perception of your situation will expand.

You will see your life as having far more potential and many more possibilities for enjoyment. You will see that controlling it is unnecessary, and that accepting the way it flows is satisfying and stimulating in ways that you never imagined were possible.

When you attempt to control your life, you find that you also have to try to control others where their lives interact with yours. This demands enormous energy and concentration which prevents you from observing the big picture — life itself. When you start to accept the flow of life — allowing it to happen at its own pace — everything becomes easier and more relaxed, and you begin to discover that you do indeed have plenty of time to do what you want to do. You will find yourselves far more frequently doing what you want to do, instead of what you need to do.

Yes, there will still be things you need to do, but you will find yourselves doing them when you want to, instead of being driven to do them, and you will find enjoyment and satisfaction in the doing, rather than pressure, irritation, and anxiety.

Life, while you are living it, is your life to live — as you want to live it. And everyone else has that right too. As more and more of you accept this, harmony in every kind of human relationship — intimate, personal, business, casual — will grow and flourish quite brilliantly, and relationship-problems at every level of society will be solved far more easily and effectively as it becomes apparent that all are striving for the same results, i.e., to make winners out of everyone.

God wants you all to win. . . and you all will; there are no losers because that is not part of God's plan.

Humanity lives in a free-will environment that it can influence enormously, and that is how it became possible to create situations of loss, pain, anger, resentment, distrust, and disillusionment. However your environment is but a small part of Creation, and when you are ready, even within that limited environment you will find that you can experience the divine environment of love, peace, harmony, and infinite possibility for delight and wonder.

Disharmony is a thought form, a belief system that you have made for yourselves, and you can and you will change it. There is no need for it, and many of you are at last becoming aware of this and refusing to accept it. When you all do, it will dissolve completely. And this is going to happen far sooner than most of you expect.

So start creating harmony now. . . and create it continuously wherever you are, and be delighted and amazed at the results.

Ө   Ө   Ө

63   Erring is human — and so is anger!

You do live in an age of great change, both on the physical and on the spiritual levels. As people become more aware and concerned about what meaning their earthly lives have for them, they also become more concerned about the meaning of life itself, and are thus opening themselves to the possibility of the

116

existence of spiritual realms. They want guidance and knowledge about things spiritual, and they search widely for information.

Many people have set themselves up as guides, or have founded churches to provide for this need, and much discrimination is needed to avoid being sucked into an organization that claims, in the most beguiling way, to offer answers, when the real intent of the founder is frequently power and control, and of course material wealth.

Every single human has her own collection of spiritual guides in the spiritual realms, waiting to assist her when called upon. And every human has the power and the ability to go within to find that assistance and guidance. Everything you need to advance along your spiritual path is available to you if you will go within. Release your preconceptions and prejudices, quieten your thought processes, ask God for help, and then listen to the guidance you are offered.

And ask for help to release those preconceptions and prejudices that every one of you has, because they are your biggest blocks to your spiritual growth. They make it extremely difficult for you to "hear" the advice that you are being offered. The word "hear" can be exchanged for "sense", "feel", "see", or "know", in so far as most of you do not actually hear voices, but you do get a very definite felt sense about new ideas or understandings that appear to drop into your awareness and which you know are right and make total sense. This sense of knowing is confirmed by the feeling of love and acceptance that flows in at the same moment.

There will never be demands, or suggestions to judge, condemn, or punish others, only a sense of understanding, compassion, and love. This may be difficult to accept at first, particularly if someone comes to mind who has hurt or offended you. The thoughts of punishing or getting even may come to mind, and if you dwell on them (which is often very tempting!), you will find it very difficult to sense your guidance.

Ask for help to release these distracting thoughts, and then just let them go. Ask also for help to recall and then release remembered painful and damaging experiences from throughout your lives, and to understand the pain and confusion of those who hurt you so that you may forgive them.

If you do not forgive others, they retain an emotional charge on you, and you become angry when you think of them. This is very stressful and prevents you from relaxing, from entering your place of peace where you can experience God's unconditional Love and acceptance of you. When you are angry with even one person you are not open to receive love, because the anger consumes you and takes all your attention. In human terms your anger may well seem totally justifiable; but your anger damages, drains, and distracts you from your life purpose, and it is essential that you release it. You know how much better it feels when you are not angry, so when you become angry, attempt to release it as soon as possible.

At first this will be difficult because of your feeling of justification for your anger. However, you also know from experience that after expressing your anger at others you frequently feel remorse, either because you know that you reacted too strongly, or because you receive information that you did not have at the time which shows you that your anger was indeed out of place.

Seeking justification is in itself stressful and self-damaging because you have to take great pains to ensure that you are always right — which you know is impossible — and therefore, of course, other people have to be made wrong, so you use much energy trying to hide and bury your errors.

To err is human. . . so allow! Release your anger, your sense of justification, and start to enjoy life. It is difficult at first, especially if you have obtained satisfaction from expressing your seemingly justifiable anger in the past. It leaves an empty space which you are strongly tempted to fill with more of same because you have a right to be angry! So leave it vacant. . . and, slowly, you will find yourselves more at peace, calmer, and happiness will flow into your lives as more space becomes available.

Θ   Θ   Θ

64   All is ready for this new reality to fall instantly into place

Much is presently occurring on Earth that is frightening and unsettling for humanity. Thoughts of war and plans for war are in the air, and very many of you are picking up on these thoughts, dwelling on them, and so giving them more energy. It is difficult for you not to plug in. Awareness of these negative energies is one thing, but dwelling on them, worrying about them, and allowing your anxieties to grow only gives them more power, more substance.

It is essential that you hold the light and intend to be love-filled for all humanity, acting as a conduit for the divine energies that are truly pouring down abundantly on Planet Earth at this time.

Relax, meditate, pray, and intend that these divine energies bring about a sea-change in all human relations, and assist the divine plan for humanity to bring the new age of peace, harmony, compassion, healing, and love rapidly into being. All is ready for this new reality to fall instantly into place. Strengthen your intent and your desire for it to happen, so that the presently dissipating energies of fear and hate will just suddenly dissolve, like morning mist, and allow the new divine Reality to comp- letely envelop Planet Earth.

All this has been planned for a very long time, and now the moment for completion is close at hand. The violence that you see around the world at this time is truly a final eruption, a last fling before the vast majority of humanity is swept up into the most unimaginably powerful environment of love, respect, acceptance, and recognition of each others' divinity, of each others' Oneness with All That Is.

When this realization pours into the awareness of each of you, you will be filled with the most inconceivable joy. Right now you may well feel, "How could this possibly occur, when we see mostly hate, violence, distrust, and fear all around us"; but once this awakening into full consciousness happens — very soon indeed now, in your earthly sense of time — you will understand how it came to pass.

And you will delight in the power of the divine — in which you of course share — to create and bring into existence this most wonderful reality for which you have all been waiting and longing. It is shortly to happen. Hold and strengthen your intent, and continue to be wonderfully effective conduits through which the divine energies flow.

Ѳ   Ѳ   Ѳ

65   How you experience living your life is completely your choice

Your life is an ongoing work of art that gives great pleasure to God and to all in the spiritual realms. If God enjoys it, then surely you should too. If you are not truly enjoying your lives you need to look inwards to identify the areas, the perceptions, and the activities that are blocking your enjoyment.

As you identify the parts that displease you, ask your guides for help to release and dissolve them. It may just be that your perception of an activity or lifestyle is unnecessarily limited, and once you begin to see the bigger picture, you will come to accept and enjoy it. On the other hand a change in activity or lifestyle may be required, and your guides will offer you ideas that will enable you to see new and more appropriate areas of opportunity that you can access and play with.

Remember always that life is a game that you, with great wisdom and foresight, chose to play. Games are meant to be fun, otherwise they would not be played. So if your game is not fun it means that you are not playing it the way you intended. In that case go inwards, seek assistance from your willing guides, and discover the changes that you need to make.

It is no use arriving at the top of a magnificent ski slope and planning to descend on roller skates! You will have to go back and get your skis, as attempting to go down on the roller skates would be a most unpleasant experience, and to persist with the attempt would only serve to increase the frustration and dissatisfaction.

However if you had arrived at the slope with a paraglider, you could possibly have made a very satisfactory compromise and flown down! So do make sure to investigate all your options when you are planning a change. Grabbing at the first one that you become aware of will often work for you after a fashion. But it is much better to review all available solutions before making your choice.

Your intuition is a most marvelous treasure trove of ideas and resources that is always available. Practice listening to it and playing with the ideas it offers you, because it will provide you with many creative scenarios that you can apply to your life. A flow of creative ideas provides great energy and enthusiasm for living your life, so let them flow and be astounded by the increased motivation and enthusiasm you will find you have for living.

Depression and lack of spontaneity are sure signs that you are not hearing and responding to the multitude of positive ideas with which your intuition is attempting to provide you. You may well have locked yourself very firmly into an extremely narrow view of life beyond or around which you refuse to look.

This is of course a choice that you have every right to make, but the lack, limitation, and dissatisfaction that you then experience are also your choices! No one else forces you to experience life as limiting, unsatisfactory, or miserable. How you experience your life is a result of choices that you make in every moment.

People in extreme poverty, without the services that you in the so-called civilized world consider to be absolutely essential for basic survival, can and do have tremendously fulfilling, satisfying, and happy lives. And you are all aware of people who can avail themselves of anything material that they wish who live in heart-breaking misery.

Life truly is what you make of it. So do not wait for someone else to provide you with opportunity, security, or happiness, because they cannot! You create your life in every moment, happy or miserable, exciting or boring, abundant or lacking. And the way you experience it is the way you choose to experience it.

If you associate with people who choose to be unhappy, you will be very much affected by the energies with which they surround themselves, and you will then find it difficult to be happy

yourself. Also, if you are happy, they will resent you and possibly attempt to show you why you too should be unhappy.

Conversely, if you associate with happy people, you will find it
much harder to be unhappy, and they will attempt to raise your
spirits if you are glum.

Choose carefully with whom you choose to associate, as you
know that people's energies, electromagnetic fields and moods,
mingle and interact, affecting how each of them feels. You are
not an isolated individual, and you cannot be unaffected by the
amazing energy currents that swirl constantly around you.

Ө   Ө   Ө

66   Openness of mind allows awareness to develop

Openness of mind allows awareness and mindfulness to develop
and grow, causing judgment, blame, bigotry, hypocrisy, and
blindness to fall away. The meaning of everything becomes
increasingly deeper, fuller, more complex (yet in ways much
simpler), and very beautiful.

Narrowness of outlook hides beauty and obstructs creative
endeavor, so that those who cling to it — through fear, of course
— severely limit their chances of experiencing a joy-filled life.

The set ways of the narrow-minded are self-defeating, because
they strengthen and increase the number of fears that these attitudes are intended to prevent and remove. Fear feeds on itself.
Release it and it just falls away. Hold onto it, dwell on it, and it
grows and expands profusely, nourished by the attention it
receives.

There is truly nothing to fear, because nothing occurs in your
lives that you are unable to deal with. Apparent inability to deal
with a situation, a crisis, or life itself is a very conscious choice a

person makes in total freedom. Choices and alternatives are always available.

The decision to avail or not to avail, to choose or not to choose, are the sole responsibility of each individual. Choosing not to be aware or mindful makes it much more difficult to accept choice or opportunity in your lives. It encourages you to nurture fear and establishes a victim mentality that creates a mental and emotional prison for you, from which it becomes increasingly difficult to break out. The more effectively this prison is constructed, the more insistent becomes the belief that to leave it would be disastrous , because it is so safe inside and, therefore, so dangerous outside.

ɵ ɵ ɵ

67   Doubts and disbelief are safety devices

It is quite natural and normal as a human to experience doubts and disbelief; they are safety devices, if you will, because on the Earth plane all is not clear, and wise and practical discernment is a necessary prelude to any project or activity.

Allow these thoughts and feelings their space, their moment, and then release them — with love. If they are valid — because you have acknowledged them by allowing them — they will provide subtle warnings or information, enabling you to proceed appropriately in any situation.

The point is not to be overwhelmed with fear or acute anxiety that freezes you in your tracks. Just be prepared for difficulties that may arise, and know that your life path has been exceedingly well planned, and that everything you need to cope with difficulties and problems is always available. If it is not immediately apparent, relax. . . go to your place of inner peace, and allow whatever concerns you to come to the surface of your awareness. Then ask for guidance.

You may well not receive an instantaneous answer, but your request has been heard, and the appropriate steps for you to take will become apparent.

Deep within you know this, and by going to your place of inner peace you allow this knowledge to seep into your awareness. As it does so, you will feel peaceful and relaxed, confident that all will turn out precisely as it should, in accordance with your Father's divine Will— which of course is also yours.

You are divinely loved and cared for. Everything that happens in your life has a divine purpose. So allow yourselves to understand and accept that. . . and you will experience the peace and trust that will enable you to operate most successfully in the midst of even the greatest difficulties, because you know that you are divinely guided in every moment, and that the difficulties that you are encountering have been chosen with great wisdom for the lessons with which they will present you.

As I have said before, there are no accidents; everything is planned. The only unknown — and this can be quite a surprise — is your response. Your free will is king. It is up to you in every moment how you respond in every moment.

Therefore, prayer and meditation are an essential part of your lives. They teach you to listen to and understand your divine guidance, and enable you to practice acting upon it. When you do so, your situational responses will be far wiser, and your lessons far more easily learned. If you do not meditate and pray regularly, you will not be well prepared to deal with the problems with which your lessons present you, and you may well make inappropriate responses that necessitate repetition of the lesson.

So do meditate and pray. Listen carefully, and follow your Father's divine guidance, allowing your lives to flow far more smoothly for you.

Θ   Θ   Θ

68   Major change is essential and inevitable

Your time spent on the Earth plane is an opportunity for spiritual growth of a kind that is not possible when you are present in the spiritual realms. The fact that you cannot remember who you truly are, or what your relationship is to your divine Creator means that you have no preconceived notions about your origin or your destiny. Consequently, you can grow and change very quickly, even though it appears to you that change is difficult and fraught with uncertainties.

As you live your earthly lives, opportunities and challenges that you prepared for yourselves before you became human appear before you, demanding your attention. Each of them was carefully planned so that its arrival on your life path would occur precisely at the moment that was most appropriate for the lesson that it would provide. The main lesson is that you are a part of, permanently connected to, and totally contained within the Creator, All That Is — as is air in the atmosphere or water in the ocean. But you also always retain your individuality, your sense of self, while contained and remaining within the Whole. When you truly know and understand this without any doubts or uncertainties whatsoever — and you will — then you will know that that your will and the divine Will are the same — always.

To know and to experience this is to move into full consciousness — the state that is your right and your heritage. Humanity

126

A Saul Book

is moving very rapidly indeed towards this indescribably wonderful, divine state of existence. You do not need to experience further Earth lives to learn the required lessons; you have already done that.

At this moment most of humanity is experiencing a very strong sense that major change is inevitable and essential for the good of the planet — and you are not being misled. Change is most definitely in the air and is very palpable. Your task, in these last few moments of the old order, is to desire and intend for these changes to take place, to pray for them, and to believe that they are about to happen — and truly they are!

By immersing yourselves totally in this intent whenever you pray, meditate, or just relax into your own personal place of peace, you greatly enhance and intensify the divine energies that are pouring down most abundantly on your planet at this time. The moment for this most wondrous and gigantic change in your Earth environment and in your individual abilities to perceive and share in it is almost upon you. Enjoy the remaining period before the change by relaxing into a state of joyful and excited expectancy, knowing that your divine Father will very soon deliver, in the most glorious abundance and diversity, everything that He has always promised.

There will be gifts galore, of a variety and magnificence that in your present human state you cannot possibly imagine. Your joy will be complete, and any sense of fear, anxiety, doubt, or disbelief will be blown away as you return to your natural divine state of being — at one with, enveloped by, and totally contained within the divine One, where there is only joy.

The moment is approaching. . . so prepare yourselves for infinite, perpetual delight and wonder. It is your right and you will receive it — very soon.

127

The discomforts, the inadequacies, and any sense of loneliness or abandonment will be instantly banished. You will not remember experiencing such sensations as you awaken into the state of full consciousness in which you have and always will exist — a state that is your heritage and your home, your true and eternal Home, but of which you have been temporarily unaware.

In this state of unawareness it has been immensely difficult for you to have faith in God's infinite Love for you, or to believe that a form of existence that provides perpetual happiness exists — a state that has been lovingly prepared for you, and to which you are about to return.

But nevertheless, you have continued to believe and to pray, despite all the misinformation and confusion that has surrounded you for so long, and you are shortly to be fully rewarded. The divine moment of intense brilliance is almost upon you, so enjoy these last few moments, knowing that very soon your happiness will be complete.

Θ   Θ   Θ

69   Go with your inner guidance

As you are well aware your prayers are always heard and answered. But you do need to practice listening. And this is frequently difficult for you as stray thoughts pop into your heads and distract you. Let them pass. . . and continue to listen with patience and in peace, knowing that everything occurs at precisely the right time.

You will hear your Creator's answer. Often it comes as an intuitive urge or nudge. Be ready for it. Sometimes it may seem quite illogical, and yet something tells you it is not. Go with your

128

inner sense, your guidance. It feels right — even though you cannot understand why.

As you learn to trust it, you will find life flowing more smoothly for you, allowing you to increase your awareness of, and your trust in, your inner guidance, your intuition. It is a gift from God to assist you on the Earth plane; so use it to the full — that is what it is for. As you practice listening and responding positively to your intuition, it will become clearer, more definite. You will find yourself doubting it far less often, and responding positively to it more frequently. It will bring you peace and tranquility as you realize that by allowing yourselves to be guided by it you are aligning your will with God's.

When you chose to incarnate, it was your intent to do the divine Will in every moment. However, on Earth as a human, you experience many distractions and seductions that make it difficult to be aware of your heaven-sent guidance. You have seen and experienced something similar in the physical world when you have addressed someone who is engrossed in a task or a book, or is deep in thought. The person you address does not respond. You address him again, and he looks up, confused, becomes aware of your presence, and responds.

And so it is with your intuition, your inner guidance. It attempts to get your attention; sometimes it succeeds. But at other times it does not because "you are making so much noise," your attention is elsewhere, very focused in the physical world.

That is why setting time aside daily just to be quiet, silent, listening in the now moment is so important. Doing this allows your intuition to slip into your awareness. This is when an inspiration is most likely to occur, and you say "ah-ha" to yourself, as a solution to some problem presents itself to you. The more frequently you allow yourselves to enter that quiet inner space, the more effective you become at it, until you find yourselves allowing the quiet and peace to envelop you whenever you need assistance with a problem, so that the solution can pop into your awareness effortlessly. It is a most satisfying way to live, allowing the divine Will to guide you in every moment, and knowing that you will not be misled.

An outcome may surprise you, because it is totally unexpected, and yet you will find that it is always completely appropriate. And so your trust in this divine gift strengthens, and you know that in every moment — if it is your desire and intent — you are always most appropriately guided. Trust your loving Father and know that He always delivers exactly what is needed at precisely the most opportune moment.

Θ   Θ   Θ

70   A flood of openness to new ideas is sweeping across the planet

Life for humanity is becoming far more meaningful as people listen to their guidance — their inner knowing or intuition — and start responding to it positively. It has always been available, but has generally remained unheard beneath the noise of loudly talking egos.

The ego has two modes of operation: defense, and attack; and both are very noisy. But people all over the planet are becoming increasingly aware that the confrontational mode of behavior in which the ego operates, which has been practiced by so many for so long, is self-defeating and self-destructive. They are starting to search for better ways, and as the ego can offer no help here, they are beginning to take the preliminary steps necessary to quieten it.

As they begin to experience moments of quietness, when the mind is still and silent, they are surprised at the sense of peace it brings. This encourages them to seek further quiet moments in their minds and in their environments. After a while they are doing it on a regular basis, and once they have adjusted to the peace and tranquility this provides, they start to become aware of their intuition or inner guidance, and what it offers them.

New ideas for dealing with people in a more positive fashion slip into their awareness. They try some of them, find that they are most effective, and that when they use them and develop the skills that the ideas suggest, they discover that confrontational situations occur far less frequently.

There has been a very marked increase over the last few decades in the number of people seeking peace and quietness as a respite from the constant ego-chatter they normally experience. This is readily apparent to anyone who visits book stores or surfs the web and sees the big increase in the amount of spiritual books now being published. People need help, guidance, and advice, and so these become available in growing quantities as people seek more actively and frequently.

The tide of ignorance, and the judgment that rides with it, has turned, and a flood of openness to new ideas and information is sweeping across the planet and flowing into even the most inaccessible nooks and crannies, where arrogance and the refusal to look at new ideas have been so firmly embedded for so long.

This spirit of inquiry and openness is cleaning out old dogma and outworn, ineffective patterns of thought and behavior, thus clearing the way for new growth — of ideas, of curiosity, and of acceptance and respect for others.

These are sprouting with the exuberance of new shoots in this

Our Divine Destiny

divine spring that is melting and thawing the winter ice that has kept humanity frozen in inflexibility and denial for far too long.

This explosion of growth and vitality as the ice finally melts is a joy to behold.

So open your hearts and your minds and allow it to take root in each one of you, filing you with vitality, enthusiasm, and love for the divine creation of which you are each an essential and irreplaceable constituent.

ϴ ϴ ϴ

71   Be on the lookout for others who are following similar paths to your own

Your continuing growth in awareness, love, and acceptance is a joy to behold. Realize that what is happening to you is also happening to many other wonderful beings inhabiting Planet Earth at this time; and many of you are meeting and seeing the love and beauty that shines forth from one another. This recognition, acceptance, and unconditional love that you offer each other is vital to your own growth and to the well-being and healing of your planet. Be aware and on the lookout for others who are following similar paths to your own. Welcome them into your homes and communities, and so assist them in their growth into awareness; they will assist you greatly in a similar fashion.

Peace, harmony, love, acceptance, and above all forgiveness will lead you onwards rapidly, taking the planet and all she supports with you into the Golden Age of harmony, happiness, and delight that is dawning. Do not allow disagreements and misunderstandings to drive wedges between you, damaging —

sometimes most severely — the personal and community relationships that you have expended so much loving energy to build.

Do not be offended by others' words or actions; show them love and acceptance, and release your fears. This will lead to extremely rapid healing of emotional hurts, and a great strengthening of these wonderful and most essential relationships that are forming all over your planet at this time.

Healthy, loving relationships, forged out of acceptance and forgiveness, lead to high levels of interpersonal and intercommunal understanding, allowing creative ventures (and adventures!) to be undertaken most successfully, due to the confident and congenial cooperation that occurs under these conditions.

Your intent — the intentions of each one of you — is incredibly strong and vibrant, like new spring growth in a fertile environment. Maintain and strengthen your intentions. Be aware of them in the background of your consciousness at all times (skiing, brushing your teeth, paying bills, in traffic jams, on the subway, just everywhere), and know that they will be brought into existence just as you desire, filling the planet with even more loving and healing energy, and accelerating her transition into the new Golden Age towards which you are all aiming so enthusiastically.

This age that is dawning for you now is long overdue in your terms, as so many of you have for so long resisted the wonderful changes that God has been offering you in unconditional Love since the beginning of time.

Now that you are finally awakening to love and awareness, the marvelous benefits of His plan are about to burst upon you in an almighty flood of brilliant consciousness, and you will know and experience His infinite Love for and delight in you, His glorious children.

You will initially be quite overwhelmed with the feeling and the experience of how much you are loved and accepted by Him. This overwhelm will lead quickly to a sense of bliss and delight that, in your present, still unawakened state, you are totally incapable of imagining. So keep strengthening your intent for the Golden Age to arrive, bringing with it everything that your hearts could wish for, and far more besides. Open your hearts even further and accept the wondrous gifts that your Father is offering you — right now, as He always has — and they will be yours to take and enjoy.

The Christmases enjoyed by the small children of doting parents and grandparents under magnificently decorated Christmas trees are as nothing in comparison to what all of you most glorious souls are about to experience.

Ɵ   Ɵ   Ɵ

72   Much acceptance is necessary if people are to maintain their relationships

Life's trials and tribulations, which we were addressing earlier, will continue to be of great importance for much of humanity, as Earth moves into her new environment of increasing consciousness. The energy changes that this entails affect every living being — and affect them all differently, and to a greater or lesser extent — which creates considerable confusion in their lives and relationships. Much patience, love, and acceptance are necessary if people are to maintain and improve their relationships. So it is essential for them to intend to live in a relaxed state of beingness, and to keep this intent firmly in mind in everyday living, and to ask constantly for help with it during their absolutely essential daily meditation.

In what you call the industrialized nations people tend to focus largely on what is wrong in their lives, or on what they think needs to be improved, instead of seeing, enjoying, and giving thanks for all the good things — and there are many of them.

This unbalanced focus on the negative attracts energies of disruption and disharmony into one's environment, whereas focusing on the positive in one's life (while retaining an accepting awareness of the less satisfactory aspects) leads to a much more joyful and harmonious state of existence. This provides copious energy that greatly assists in the positive and harmonious solutions to problems, which in other, more negative states of being become, by choice, insoluble.

Give-and-take — the sharing of assets, joys, and chores — works wonders. Demanding and insisting on your rights, as you see them (and generally it is only you who sees them in precisely this light), leads to disharmonious confrontation that achieves little, and which may well end up destroying whatever may have already been accomplished.

Put your daily meditation to good use by giving thanks for your truly wonderful state of existence, and for the gifts that that state continuously provides for you. Then bring to mind your heartfelt desires and intents and ask for help to achieve them. And ask that all those whom you know and love be blessed with the energies that they need to live life fully as they — in unity with their full selves and their Creator — have always intended.

Sending out these loving energies in your daily meditation is incredibly powerful and effective, and lightens and uplifts your whole neighboring environment.

73 By changing yourselves you will change creation

Over the next few years — approximately 8–10 Earth years — there will be many, many changes to the environment of Planet Earth, as part of the immense healing process that is in progress at this time. Humanity has and is still causing much damage to Earth, your home, and part of the divine plan is for the Earth to be fully healed and returned to a state of pristine vigor; and that also goes for all the life forms she supports.

All diseases will be cured, and the causes of disease will be removed. All entities who reside on Earth, and are ready, will be raised to the state of full consciousness, and no longer will one species prey on another. This great series of changes will occur over the next few years.

As to sub-surface living (beautiful holographic environments beneath the Earth's surface), this is certainly possible. However, it is by no means certain that that will happen, for it may well not become necessary because the healing of the planet may be achieved without making the surface of the planet temporarily uninhabitable.

The more actively those of you who are becoming spiritually aware can hold an intent and a vision of planetary healing and renewal with minimal further damage and disorder, the more strongly does that become the reality that is happening. So keep praying, meditating, and intending that a beautiful, peaceful, and smooth transition occur — and make it happen.

God loves every part of His creation. And on Planet Earth He has given freedom for development to occur as desired by the inhabitants. If you – the collective – desire and intend it to happen through violence and destruction, then it will. If you desire it to happen beautifully and peacefully, then it will. Or, maybe you intend for it to happen as a blend of the two.

Your prayers and intentions are what create your environment, and the environment that you have created across your planet reflects humanity's intentions: loving and peaceful in some areas, angry and violent in others. Realize that every single person's intent has a very definite effect. So decide in every moment what you truly desire, and intend it powerfully in every moment to bring it about.

There are others from outside your solar system who are close by and desirous of helping you, but until the number of you wishing and intending to accept their help becomes large enough, they can only send love, watch over you, and offer advice to those of you who are open to receive it. When you ask, in sufficient numbers, for their very advanced (by your stand-ards) and non-violent technical assistance, they will be only too happy to provide it.

When they do. . . and they will, because more and more of you are seeking advanced technological and spiritual assistance, with increasing strength of intent, you will be amazed and enchanted by the beauty, effectiveness, and simplicity of their technology.

So once again, I cannot stress sufficiently how important your prayers, your meditations, and your intentions are. Remember that you chose to be here at this time to help with Planet Earth's transition to a much higher level of spirituality – one that grows from unconditional love and wisdom. You have the tools and you have the skills to do what you came to do. By meditating — that is, relaxing, praying, being peaceful, being hopeful, being optimistic, being open, and being aware — and allowing yourselves to be your selves, you will bring about this most marvelous transition that God has planned, and that every single one of you have agreed and deeply desired to assist in bringing into being. So cease worrying anxiously and angrily about what is being done, or not being done, and put your spiritual tools to work, as was your intent before you incarnated as humans, and bring the divine plan to fruition as only you can.

You took on a human life in order to do this – not to watch others, judge them, and find them wanting. So cease this unhelpful behavior; let divine Love pour abundantly into and through you, so that you love, encourage, accept, and forgive others, and by so doing, teach them to do likewise.

You know that the only effective way to teach is by example, so if you want others to change, change yourselves. Be the example that teaches by inspiring. Let judgment, anger, resentment, and condemnation fall away. Then your innate God-given power will align most powerfully with your loving intent.

By changing yourselves you will truly change creation!

Θ Θ Θ

74   The most wonderful changes are to come about in the environment that humanity inhabits

The Creator's divine plan is rolling smoothly along, as it always does, because that is His Intent – which is always perfectly achieved. The last few loose ends, enabling completion of the current stage, will be tied up very soon, allowing the most wonderful changes to come about in the environment that humanity inhabits.

This environment means not only the physical aspects of which all are generally aware, but also the spiritual, psychic, emotional, psychological, and philosophical aspects. In fact, every aspect of human life will experience a great shift, a great change in the way it is experienced. The changes that are to happen very shortly will be truly astounding for humanity, who will experience them instantly at the moment they occur.

One moment "normal" human life will be in progress, then suddenly — literally within the blink of an eye — all will have changed. People will rub their eyes in disbelief a couple of times, as they "awaken" to their stunning new environment and realize immediately with untold delight that they are Home, that they have arrived at the heavenly destination which they have been yearning and seeking for so long.

The joy will be contagious as all recognize quite clearly what has happened, and why. Fear, pain, worry, anxiety, and any other sense of lack, inadequacy, or dissatisfaction will dissolve instantly and be forgotten. It will be as though those unhappy sensations had never existed; and there will be no unhappy memories of any sort at all to disturb the divine harmony that envelops your whole environment.

Everything that you experience from this moment forward will be wonderful and bliss-filled, as never before experienced by humans in the Earth plane. You will remember and identify most joyfully with your origins in the divine spiritual realms, knowing that that is where you were so joyfully created, where you have always existed, and where you will continue to exist in an ever-increasing state of ecstasy, rejoicing eternally, forever, and without end. You will indeed have come Home for good, and you will know the experiences that you underwent were by your own choice, in order to magnify infinitely the joy of existence in God's divine creation. The moment is almost upon you, so prepare to enjoy and enjoy and enjoy!

Θ Θ Θ

75 Enormous power and energy are available to you

As life progresses for each member of the human race, spiritual growth occurs on a much larger and more magnificent scale than you can possibly imagine. Remember, you all chose to experience life as humans because you knew what great opportunities the human condition offers for spiritual development. You also knew that you would be without any knowledge or awareness of who you truly are, as you underwent the experience.

The unpleasantness, the joy, the catastrophes and disasters, the delights and satisfactions that fill your own lives — or that you observe occurring to others — are all part of the plan you created to enable your spiritual growth to move forward as rapidly and as appropriately as possible.

You are all learning enormously valuable lessons from the human life experience, and what you have learned and what you have become spiritually will truly amaze you when you return to these realms and remove your earplugs and blinkers!

By meditating daily, and by frequent, short periods during the day of withdrawal into your place of inner peace, you allow God's energies to flow through you, giving you the strength and perseverance to follow your chosen life path. Enormous power and energy are available to help you on your path, but you must ask for it, and you must open your hearts to allow it in. Without your constant ongoing permission, allowing God and your guides and friends in our realms to help you, no help can reach you.

If you stubbornly refuse to accept help, that refusal will be totally honored. And yet we frequently see souls desperate and despairing, longing for help and guidance, but refusing to ask for it. . . or asking and then refusing to accept it.

Our Divine Destiny

The refusal, the inability to accept help often comes from feelings of pride, shame, guilt, fear, anxiety, or unworthiness on the part of the soul entity. All of these feelings are quite natural because they are part of your humanness, and you have them — along with all your other feelings — to help you and guide you. But they are not meant to control you. Nevertheless, many of you allow them to do just that. By retreating to your place of inner peace for brief periods regularly during the day, and quieting your mind from its unceasing chattering distractions, you allow yourselves the opportunity to observe yourselves as humans experiencing the human condition. You can then see your feelings and emotions for what they are: tools to enable you to live with grace and elegance, not manipulative powers that control you.

They can never control you. However. . . many of you play a game in which you see yourselves as victims controlled by your feelings and emotions, and you react to them without thought or consideration, seemingly at their mercy, quite helpless to do otherwise, and not, apparently, in any way responsible for your actions. And as long as you wish to play this game, you are free to do so.

Eventually the pain and discomfort increases to a level that you find unacceptable; inside you something breaks and you have to take action. As humans, that action is likely to be an attempt to find a new way to play the same old game, lapse into some degree of insanity by shutting down the small amount of self-awareness that you had begun to permit yourselves, or even to allow your body to become ill and die.

Alternatively. . . you may decide that you truly have spent more than enough time playing this no-longer-satisfying game, whereupon you will awaken into awareness of your own self-sabotage. Then you will seek, find, and accept the help that you desire and that you need in order to enable you to move forward and once more take responsibility for the free will that you have always had — however you may have chosen to use it.

The sooner you permit this break, this interruption, this true self-awareness to occur, the sooner you will start following your chosen life path, amazed by what you see around you that you have chosen to create, and enabling you and all those with whom you interact to move rapidly forward as you have always intended.

Ө   Ө   Ө

76 "Party time"

Right now, much is happening in the heavenly realms that would astound you. It is truly a case of "party time"! Humanity's move into full consciousness is almost upon you, and we are in a state of joy as we watch this momentous divine event approaching.

The planetwide prayer and meditation holding that intent is continuous and increasing in power. At every moment groups and individuals all over your beloved planet are praying and meditating for peace, harmony, and abundance. Those prayers are being received with great joy by our Creator. He loves you all infinitely, and He will shortly deliver – as requested.

Because of your state of free will, a large number of you have been required to hold the intent and pray for this moment with all the power and intensity possible.

Vast numbers of humans have yet to awaken, but deep within themselves they desire and intend to do so. Therefore, practically all of humanity desires, intends, and wills most powerfully to reawaken into full consciousness – your natural state of existence.

Over the eons, this desire has been growing, spreading, and intensifying as all humans have allowed this most wonderful divine seed to be planted within them. As more of you have awakened to the desire for peace, harmony, and unconditional love, you have nurtured these seeds and encouraged them to grow and develop within you.

At first the growth was slow and steady to allow a strong base, foundation, or root system to develop, in order to support the most magnificent blossoming of unconditional love throughout humanity. The foundations are now most firmly established, and the most beautiful flowering is about to burst forth in a brilliant and glorious display.

These flowers are perpetual and ever-lasting, and they will continue to flourish and develop into ever more glorious versions of themselves for their own radiant pleasure. In doing this they delight our Creator by being exactly and precisely what they are. And all of creation shares in that joy, which will grow unceasingly, intensifying every moment of joy as it occurs.

And it is all about to occur! So intensify your prayers and meditation. Allow the divine abundance to suffuse you utterly, and come alive in this most amazing and inspiring Golden Age of coming together in peace, harmony, and bliss – which God's infinite, unconditional Love provides.

ϴ   ϴ   ϴ

77   Ill health is a sign that you are not paying attention to your inner guidance

Health – good health – is very important, because when you

have it, it is much easier for you to deal with life's many and varied experiences. Sickness, disease, and general ill health (physical or psychological) are signs that you are not paying attention but are instead blocking out or refusing to hear or listen to your inner guidance.

Every human has inner guidance available to him, and can choose to listen to it – or not. Its content and its characteristics were chosen by the individual to suit the unique experience that he would undergo during his human life. When ill health occurs, an individual seeks healing and in so doing, seeks causes or reasons for his illness.

Your culture has taught you that when you are ill you need a doctor or healer to assist you to recover. And very frequently these people can and do help you, but your body has its own inbuilt healing and repair system, and if you will listen to your inner guidance you will learn how best to assist it in its healing process.

If you truly listened to and acted on your inner guidance you would experience far fewer diseases, illnesses, and damaging accidents to your physical bodies, and far fewer serious psychological and emotional disturbances.

All the pain and discomfort that you experience is telling you that something is not flowing as smoothly in your lives – is not as balanced – as it should be. You may well have chosen certain illnesses or accidents so that certain aspects of the way you live would be brought forcefully to your attention. But until you have identified those aspects and balanced them correctly, you will not be able to heal yourselves properly. You may heal one illness, but another will occur if you do not do the inner work, the spiritual work that you came on Earth to do.

It is essential to listen to your inner guidance without prejudice or expectation so that you are fully open to — and not dismissive of — the advice and information it has to offer you.

It does require some practice to be able to listen to your guidance, which is why frequent periods when you relax and still your mind during the day are most necessary. On the whole, your various social philosophies – whether cultural, religious, scientific, educational – have taught and encouraged you from a very early age not to give credence to your inner knowing, your gut feelings, and your instincts. Yet the vast majority of you can recall times when you followed – or disregarded – that inner knowing, and later discovered that it was totally valid.

So you do know deep within yourselves that it is there for you – always – and that you have only to allow yourselves access to it to make it available. Quite often you will get a sense, a feeling that you should change something in your life — in your way of doing or dealing with something — and it makes you feel quite uncomfortable or anxious; you do not want to change a process that you have followed, apparently satisfactorily, for years. You rebel, and you refuse to change. Maybe you think that it will be an admission that you were at fault, wrong, or blameworthy, and to change would shame you. But refusing to change only strengthens the feeling that you should. These refusals to accept or acknowledge guidance and information from within create blocks that make living more difficult for you, and lead to ill health.

So listen for and to your guidance. Evaluate it and the know-ledge it brings you. Then act deliberately, purposefully, and appropriately.

Changing how you do something may well cause some dis-comfort at first, due to unfamiliarity and uncertainty. But once the change becomes more habitual, that feeling will dissolve and you will notice a reduction in your stress levels, an increase in your energy and zest for life, and a most welcome ability to relax, listen to, and acknowledge that wonderful inner guidance that is always instantly available to assist you at any given moment.

ϴ   ϴ   ϴ

78   Spiritual progress on a vast and unprecedented scale awaits you all

As you allow and encourage yourselves to open into mindful awareness, I and many others who love you dearly can certainly help you with this task. This will be most valuable for you (anyone who reads this) and for all those whom you love, as they too will then be further assisted in their stalwart efforts to complete this task of awakening for themselves.

This is an essential step on the road back to full consciousness which humanity is now following, in order to allow the new Golden Age of joy and abundance to envelop not only humanity but also Planet Earth, your solar system, and the whole Milky Way Galaxy.

Spiritual growth on a vast and unprecedented scale awaits you all, and will be brought into being by ordinary everyday humans, like you, becoming increasingly aware of how your individual patterns of thought and emotion affect and alter the divine creation.

Every one of you is vitally important to the divine plan. And each one who increases her openness to the powerful healing energies flooding into your environment at this time leads to many more souls also opening up. The knock-on effect of one person opening her heart to her divine life purpose is quite

147

staggering; and if you will look, you can truly see it happening around you in many areas of the planet.

Remember that your media focuses very, very, heavily on bad news, violence, and general mayhem, and yet this is in truth a very tiny part of what is happening on your planet. The explosion in the publication of books on self-help, healing, personal growth, and spiritual development shows very clearly what truly interests and motivates people in this period leading up to the new Golden Age.

The ones who are creating the *real* news, ringing the changes and bringing in the Light, are with you in large numbers throughout your beautiful planet. You have only to allow yourselves to see, feel, hear, and immerse yourselves in the magnificent energies that you are all creating, holding, and expressing to become consciously aware of the amazing and rapid progress that humanity is making right now.

Open up, be aware, perceive, and allow yourselves to experience the wonder that surrounds and envelops you with such love, tenderness, and enthusiasm — enthusiasm for the divine plan, enthusiasm for the wondrous divine creation of which you and we in the spiritual realms are all absolutely essential parts, and enthusiasm for the living reality that is being so magnificently achieved by us all.

Give your media a miss and yourselves a break, and allow yourselves to experience the marvelous reality that is all around you in such splendid abundance.

ϴ   ϴ   ϴ

79   Achieving your aims in life can be very difficult

As you go through the day experiencing life as humans, many thoughts occur to you, some pertinent and others distracting. But a common, recurring theme runs through them all, and that is your attitude to life and your judgment of it. Is it good? Bad? Overwhelming? Unsatisfactory? Are you succeeding? Failing? Being victimized? Being ignored? And of course your attitude directly affects the way you live, carry out your activities, and relate to people.

It is good to become very aware of your general attitude to life, as opposed to the way you feel about different people, activities, and events. By becoming aware, you are able to see immediately if your attitude is in keeping with your desires and intents. If it is not, then achieving your aims becomes very difficult.

The vast majority of humans wish to be seen as kind, generous, and as having integrity, and yet many of your actions demonstrate less attractive character traits.

During your periods of relaxing meditation, it is good to look occasionally at actions you have taken and responses you have made to people to see if your intent was in alignment with the way you wish to be seen. It can be very enlightening to do this after you have renewed your intent to allow God's Love to fill your hearts and guide every thought and action. You will of course notice discrepancies.

The object of the exercise is to become aware of these discrepancies and to renew your intent to allow God's Love to fill your hearts. Do not blame yourselves — or others! – for these inappropriate thoughts or actions. Just acknowledge them and release them. As you practice this exercise daily, as you renew your intent to receive and accept God's Love, you will find yourselves behaving more and more frequently in the way you intend.

You became human to be on the fast track of personal spiritual growth and development. And so, deep within each of you, there lies an intense desire to live in the light of the Creator's divine Love, and to do His Will in every moment. Doing this exercise briefly and regularly during your periods of reflection will bring your awareness of this desire more and more clearly into focus, enabling you to live it more effectively in every moment.

Your will will become one with God's Will, and you will find that conflicting desires and intentions which may frequently have seemed intractable will simply dissolve, bringing you peace and contentment as you live more fully in the divine light of Love.

Θ   Θ   Θ

80   What you are doing is what you are meant to be doing

When you relax and meditate, you put yourselves into a state of allowing. Allowing influx of information, of love, of healing, of acceptance, of compassion etc., is an opening-up of awareness and consciousness, and this leads to rapid spiritual growth.

Everyone chooses to incarnate in order to experience spiritual growth, but many get side-tracked, and consequently their spiritual development slows to a crawl as they place their focus and awareness elsewhere. However, the growth never ceases. Every incarnation brings progress, but when you relax and meditate daily and make that time an essential part of your life experience, the amount of progress you achieve is so much greater, and the amount of feedback that you receive increases phenomenally. You feel content and at peace, and able to cope with any situation that you create for yourselves.

Your need to "be in control" drops away and you live in the moment, savoring all that is going on, content in the absolute knowledge that what you are doing is what you are meant to be doing.

You discover that reacting is something you no longer need to do; your inner knowing, your intuition guides you spontaneously, so that the right response – or lack of response – is immediately apparent to you. The stressful adrenaline-pumping, habitual reactions that take over when you are not at peace, perhaps when rushing to avoid being late or missing deadlines, no longer occur.

Relaxation and meditation are unbreakable lifelines connecting you with your Full Selves and the Creator. Do not neglect them or forget about them. Use them as they are meant to be used, and you will know that you are never alone, never abandoned, but always accompanied by the divine, loving energy that is your life force, and which will always assist you if you ask for assistance, and which will never lead you astray.

Your prayers, your meditations, your loving and healing intentions are of the utmost importance at this point in the development of all of creation. So make sure to spend as much time each day as you possibly can in this way, consciously intending that love, healing, and the Creator's divine Will be done.

You will soon enjoy and delight in the experience of bursting forth into the infinite light of Love that He has prepared for all of His creation, and in meeting once more and interacting with all the wonderful souls that you have known and loved since before time began.

Your wondrous efforts are a continuous source of delight and amazement to all of us who are watching and sending you abundant energies to help you complete this great task.

Θ   Θ   Θ

81   Meditation has great power to affect communities

As life unfolds in all its unexpected wonder, it sometimes appears to be quite unsatisfactory because events occur that in human terms seem harsh, unfortunate, and better avoided. But in truth they present great opportunities for spiritual growth, and can serve as lessons on the road to wisdom if they are seen clearly, instead of in the distorted manner in which they are reported, in order, for example, to protect the reputations and worldly interests of those who may be blamed or held responsible for them.

The intense need that humans feel to blame and condemn someone for disasters and misfortunes makes it very difficult for them to come to terms with a situation that exists, and then attempt in a spirit of honesty, integrity, and cooperation to solve those difficulties in the most effective and harmonious way possible. Clear sight and harmonious cooperation can solve any challenge if people act with honesty and integrity from their heart centers for the benefit of all, instead of trying to use a situation to benefit their own personal agendas.

Reflection and meditation assist people to make contact with their centers — their connectedness with their source — and enable them to see far more clearly what is honest and beneficial, and to recognize within themselves agendas and impulses that are divisive or ill-conceived, and that need to be discarded. It also helps them to find the strength and the courage to do this, instead of acting from motives of greed and fear, which so frequently disrupt and prevent harmonious solutions from being put into effect.

Meditation and reflection by individuals or groups, especially when carried out on a frequent and regular basis, have tremendous power to affect all in their communities and to bring to them, over time, an increasing awareness of their own personal responsibilities and a strong desire to respect and honor them.

Meditation and reflection — becoming consciously connected to the divine Source — are the most powerful and effective ways to create changes for the better in society, leading to peace, harmony, and creative solutions to all the problems and difficulties that besiege humanity.

Believe it, encourage it, demonstrate it, and enjoy the results!

Θ   Θ   Θ

82   It is God's desire that you have it all

The faith and trust of those experiencing the human condition is unbelievably wonderful to behold, even that of those who seem to have none. Remember that everyone of you is loved and cherished beyond anything you could possibly imagine. In God's plan all will be brought to a state of supreme happiness in the fantastic awareness of their total integration into the divine One. Continue in your faith and trust; you have it, even if you do not think you do and do not seem to experience it. Your continuing progress is quite amazing. And soon all will be revealed to you and experienced by you in an ecstasy of wonder and delight. It truly will!

The Creator's divine plan is for Love, Peace, and Harmony to prevail throughout the universe, throughout all of creation (which is a concept of which you can have not the slightest perception while you remain captivated and distracted by your illusory three-dimensional environment, and all that that entails) — a creation of immense proportions that will continue to grow and create and recreate itself ever more abundantly and gloriously.

And this plan, this divine strategy, is utterly unstoppable. God is with you, loving you, caring for you, preparing unimaginable wonders and delights for you, because He loves you all with such infinite fervor and intensity — as you have been told over and over, and as His prophets and messengers have demonstrated again and again. All that you have to do is to allow, and you will be swept up into the arms of His infinite loving Oneness, where all that you could ever desire awaits you.

Your free will permits you to reject His Love, all that He offers, and He will not impose upon you in any way. He accepts you all — every one of you, just as you are, perfect as He created you — and when you truly and unconditionally accept Him and allow union with Him to occur, it will. . . instantly.

It's your move! And He longs for you to make it, so that your illusions of aloneness and abandonment, confusion and loss, worthlessness and unacceptability may be gone forever. It is your illusion, and it is your right to hold on to it. But why would you want to?

Allow His Oneness to envelop you and return you to the place you have truly never left. Release your illusions of sorrow, toil, anxiety, fear, hopelessness, and despair. Allow infinite joy, wonder, and delight to be yours once more.

It is His unchanging desire that you have it all! Release your pessimism and allow Him to give it to you. The joy that you will both enjoy will be boundless and everlasting. We are all waiting to welcome you home.

Θ   Θ   Θ

83   Desires enable you to identify the direction of your life path

Your lives have been well planned to allow you to grow and develop at the rate that is most appropriate for you. Periods of apparent stagnation, during which it seems that you do nothing and achieve nothing, are very valuable periods of consolidation. During these periods a tremendous amount of internal growth and organization occurs to prepare you for your "next stage" of development – and there will always be a next stage!

You need to be patient with yourselves and allow your development to progress spontaneously and naturally. Judging yourselves – as inadequate, unacceptable, lazy, incompetent, stupid, in fact any form of self-judgment at all – just weighs you down and stifles your creativity, and this distracts you from your life paths.

So be kind to yourselves. Accept yourselves as goodhearted, decent, and deserving. Allow yourselves to recognize your desires; then honor them and permit yourselves to satisfy them.

156

The only way you can truly be yourselves – and be true to yourselves – is to recognize, honor, explore, and satisfy your true desires.

Your desires make you who you are; they drive your creative spirit and carry you easily and effortlessly along your contractual paths. You have desires to enable you to identify the life-path direction to follow, and they will not lead you astray.

Practice listening to them, by being aware at all times of your ever-present intuitive guidance, which you set up before your Earth life began so that you could always find your way. Listen to your own guidance, not to the "shoulds" that your culture and environment attempt to impose upon you.

You are (while you experience human lives) individuals with perfectly natural, characteristic desires to which you are purposefully drawn because they mark your paths. To allow yourselves to be maneuvered and manipulated by societal and cultural "shoulds" is most inappropriate and leads to dissatisfaction, stagnation, and depression. You will find yourselves unable to do anything if you allow yourselves to be inhibited by the unsuitable demands of a badly programmed conscience or an inappropriate sense of responsibility.

You are each your own person. Give yourselves permission to be you and so discover who you truly are. That is why you are alive. Allow and encourage your potential to develop. . . and enjoy your amazement at the results!

Θ Θ Θ

84 Logic and intuition together make a very good team

As you follow the life path that you have planned and chosen, and as the challenges that arise are satisfactorily solved (and without great difficulty, when you allow it), realize that there is indeed a life plan unfolding for you, just as it should.

The big difficulty for most people is to allow their life path to unfold unhindered while they, ideally, live in the present moment. Too often they put together and execute life plans without seeking inner guidance or listening to their intuition, which are then truly inappropriate for them, causing delays and meandering diversions, and even emotional blocks, which leave them feeling dissatisfied and confused. The plans may succeed admirably, and yet the person will remain disillusioned with his goals and perplexed about why he feels that way. Alternatively, they may not succeed, which leads to the same result.

For a person's life path to flow as planned, it is essential that she become aware of and respond appropriately to her inner knowing, her intuition. And of course, daily periods of reflection or meditation are essential for this awareness to strengthen and develop fully.

Inner knowing can provide a very definite sense of what the right course of action is for any given life situation. More generally, it is felt as a slight preference for one action over another – a very subtle inclination for one direction rather than another. But frequently the logical mind overrides this inner knowing with rationale, resulting in a less appropriate course of action being followed. When this happens, the person is generally left with a feeling that all is not quite as it should be.

Listen to those subtle feelings; acknowledge them and learn to trust them, and you will find life flowing more smoothly. And when you do, you will often feel a surer sense of satisfaction, although your logical mind may be telling you, "I feel better, and yet logically, the course of action I am following does not make sense. What is going on here?"

As you become more adept at operating from your inner knowing, you will find that the doubts and worries thrown up by your reasoning mind will become far less strident, although they will never cease entirely.

The logical mind has a very definite role in your life, and it begins to fulfill it very well once it starts to move into harmony with your intuition. The two together make a very good team to assist you with the life that you planned. Encourage your intuition by making room for it in your life; the resulting harmonious flow will carry you confidently along on your journey of growth and discovery.

Θ　Θ　Θ

85　Live expectantly

Full consciousness is approaching rapidly, and your joy when it arrives will be enormous and complete. God keeps all His promises – always. The moment of your enlightenment is approaching swiftly! Release your doubts and prepare for the joy that He has planned for you for so long.

Live expectantly. It is one of the most positive things you can do, as it lifts your spirits and allows larger amounts of divine energy to flow into the environment. Live from your heart center by listening to your intuition – your divine inner knowing – and then do what you really desire in each moment.

And live now. . . in each moment. . . experiencing all the things your senses bring you, rather than focusing narrowly on worries and concerns. If you allow your senses to inform you in every moment, instead of shutting them out while you focus exclusively on some chore, life will flow much more enjoyably for you.

Relish life – for it is very good.

θ θ θ

86 Living in awareness

As your awareness grows and expands and your level of cons-ciousness rises, the other activities in which you choose to engage become far more effective in assisting your spiritual growth. Everything you do is valuable and pertinent, but when you meditate and expand your awareness, a synergy develops, embracing all your activities – physical, spiritual, mental, and emotional – which brings your whole being increasingly into balance, so that your development becomes a continuous process, quite different from the erratic and disjointed progress that is all you are able to achieve before you begin to grow into awareness.

Awareness is being wide awake in the spiritual sense, open to all kinds of information from every possible source, and there-fore able to live your lives in the fullest sense possible.

Living in awareness means that you cannot claim not to have known or understood what you were doing – although of course you may not have been able to foresee the eventual conse-quences of all your actions. However, you are unable to deny or refuse responsibility for those actions, and, being fully aware, you would never wish to do that.

To know and accept that you are responsible for your lives and for the actions, or lack of actions, that are a part of those lives draws highly beneficial energies to you, which greatly assist you in identifying and following your chosen paths. It also releases energies for use that would not have been available to you if you were blocking and denying the knowledge that you, and you alone, are responsible for how you choose to live and experience your lives.

At this time, when abundant energies are cascading down on Planet Earth — to ensure that all who are attempting and intending to come into awareness have everything that they require to help them in this task — the divine Creator is observing with delight as more and more souls succeed in their task of achieving enlightenment.

The movement of souls into this state is now very rapid indeed, as each one who reaches enlightenment encourages at least another three to follow it into this joyful state. The grassroots movement into enlightenment adds a tremendous groundswell of love and healing, which pours across the planet, strengthening the intent to repair, protect, and save it from further damage and possible cataclysmic disaster.

Life is a process that transcends the experience that humanity generally believes is its reason for being. As life flows, it grows and develops in ways that are not readily apparent – ways that are in fact mostly inconceivable to the majority of humans. Lacking awareness — and for the most part lacking any desire for awareness — humans mainly drift through the life process as though asleep.

This lack of awareness leads humanity to create apparently horrendous situations for itself from which it appears there is no possible escape. Yet if humanity could open its awareness, it would not — and could not — create such corruption. And if it could look at them with awareness, it would see that they did not exist as originally experienced, but were merely interesting problems or difficulties which could and would be quickly solved in loving cooperation by those affected by them.

So open your awareness – you have it, and it is the divine

Intent that you should – and move into an era of open, loving cooperation with one another, enjoying the God-given gift of life.

There is nothing He wants more than your complete happiness – but you must claim it! To do that, you need to open your awareness fully so that you can see it, and then you can claim it, because it is your rightful and divine inheritance.

Ө Ө Ө

87   When you live "in the moment". . .

When you live "in the moment," a state of openness or awareness is much easier to cultivate. This allows you to really live your lives and know at all times that you are living, because all your senses become much sharper, more intense, and more effective. Everything seems more alive, more real.

Life truly comes alive, inspiring you, enlightening you, bringing you vastly increased energy with which to live. It is like an energy spiral that becomes more powerful and more intense the further into it you advance. How far you advance into it is up to you.

When you reach a level that suits you, you can stop and rest, take stock, and then use the energy in the way that seems most appropriate. Or, you can move back to a less intense level. The energy spiral is always there for you and will always be able to lead you further, because there is no end to it. And although you may choose to remain at any one level for any length of time, it remains your servant to use as you please.

Lack of awareness is all that keeps you from seeing it, recognizing it, and knowing that it is always present.

Practice awareness unceasingly, and you will be led inevitably to these energies. Meditation, reflection, and relaxation help you to enable and realize total awareness.

When you first experience it, you will find it stimulating and tiring. But as you increase the time you spend in awareness, the tiredness will evaporate. It's all there for you at the pace at which you choose to progress. So enjoy!

When your lives are flowing smoothly, it is easy to let your awareness slip away as you focus on what you are doing. The secret is to maintain the awareness while you focus; the two are not mutually exclusive. You just have to learn to hold onto the awareness, the openness, while you focus on the job in hand.

Ө   Ө   Ө

88   It is often satisfying to put the blame for events onto others – or God

Whatever you experience is intended. At some level, you have made choices that have brought the events that you are experiencing into your lives at this precise point.

"Accidents" and "coincidences" are *planned* occurrences, with intent and purpose, which a person has chosen in order to create opportunities for learning and growth of a specific type, at a particular point in the life process he has chosen to undergo. As you know, no one is a victim; the experience of being a victim is a choice a person makes, and if it is a choice, then by definition, a person cannot be a victim.

As the experiences a person has chosen to incarnate as a human to receive and learn from can be extremely unpleasant, it is often strangely satisfying to put the blame for events onto others – or God – and thus avoid the responsibility of coming to terms with them, or learning the lessons that, at a much higher level of existence, the individual most seriously intends to learn. This can lead to repeated incarnations with the same learning-intention in similar circumstances. Taking responsibility for your lives, once you have arrived to live them, is the most satisfactory and efficient way to evolve spiritually, and enables a person to find contentment and satisfaction in any situation.

Fear of change – frequently a cultural imposition absorbed during childhood and adolescence – is the main reason why people fail to take advantage of the experiences life lays in front of you, and this is why they need to keep repeating them.

Love drives out fear, and so a truly loving person is without fear. This is why it is imperative to love, honor, and respect your children.

One of the Ten Commandments is: Honor your father and your mother. But this is impossible unless they have shown them-selves to be honorable by honoring their children. Very fre-quently parents demand from their children the honor and respect that, out of guilt and shame, they are unable to give to themselves – and hence, others. If these parental demands for respect are not satisfied, the children are judged and punished for not doing what they are incapable of doing – for as they have never experienced people honoring one another, they have not learnt how.

What they have seen demonstrated is obeisance – the respect that is paid out of fear – and they learn to offer that. But that is unacceptable because it is transparently false, and they are once again found wanting, and punished.

So fear is taught and nurtured, and the lesson that is learned, although totally at odds with reality, is that a semblance of honor and respect is to be offered to gain a particular reward or avoid punishment. Then the words "honor" and "respect" take on a strongly pejorative association, in accordance with the hypocrisy that is demonstrated.

Loving your children honors them – to honor is to accept them for who they are – and by honoring them you demonstrate love-in-action which allows them to grow up free and fearless. When this happens, they remain alive and curious throughout their formative years, and open and receptive to new ideas and experiences which enhance their growth and creativity. This teaches them that change is interesting, exciting, and enjoyable, further enhancing their curiosity and willingness to experience change. Without change there is no growth, and fear greatly discourages change and encourages the life-denying stuffiness of the status quo.

Θ   Θ   Θ

89   You were created out of pure, loving energy

When you relax and meditate, you release much energy into your environment which flows directly and easily to where it will be of most benefit in helping to heal the planet and the sentient beings who inhabit it.

You were created out of pure, loving energy and designed to be conduits through which infinite energy could flow. For that to happen you have to be wholly open in unconditional love and acceptance, cooperating freely and willingly with your Creator. That is why you were created, and, as you are blessed with free will, it is your choice whether to cooperate or not.

Free will is an energy that may be used as the person chooses, and in using it, she learns its purpose, which is to bring her to oneness with the Divine. This learning-process can be rapid, but it normally takes a large number of incarnations before the entity learns how to allow it to flow freely as God intends. Until free flow is achieved, blockages will occur which cause problems in the form of emotional denial or a lack of awareness in the person, and which lead to psychological and physical imbalances. These then tend to take up most of her attention, leaving very little energy for spiritual progress and creativity.

Remember, every day is a good one, unless you choose to experience it as something else. It is always your choice. Everything is your choice because you have free will. But free will is something about which humanity has a very limited understanding. This is of course largely due to the condition that humanity has chosen to experience: limited awareness, limited ability, limited power, limited desires, and, above all, a desire to put limits on creation itself!

Ɵ Ɵ Ɵ

90 Directed intent is very powerful

Our communications are very much concerned with the healing of Planet Earth, humanity, and all the life forms on the planet. The constant raping of the planet must cease, and you enlightened beings who chose to be here at this time to assist in healing the planet need to awaken into awareness – if you are to do what you came here to do.

Continual intent to love, heal, forgive, accept, cooperate, and harmonize are essential for Earth's healing and full recovery into her original state of pristine beauty. So make that intent in every moment of your lives. Create an aura of love and healing around you by using your focused intent, so that it may radiate from your being, wherever you are and at all times. Be a channel of divine energies, a conduit to every part of the globe, by using your loving intent. Direct your meditation to heal all life forms on your magnificent planet, including the planet herself.

Every single life form has boundless energy, but at present it is mainly disorganized and disoriented. You, with your powerful intent when you meditate, can bring organization and direction to that energy, enabling it to be a force of great power for healing.

You have all, at one time or another, experienced the power of directed energy, either from another human being or from a holy place. All of you possess this boundless energy, and all that you have to do to direct it is to intend strongly and constantly that you will direct it – and *know* that this is so – and recreate this intent in each meditation or prayer period that you set aside as time-out from your normal daily lives. If you will do this – take time-out three or four times a day to reinforce the intent that you make and hold during your meditation – you will indeed begin to see changes that will surprise and delight you in your daily lives.

Remember that your directed intent is very powerful, even if at first you get no sense of this. So make your intent firmly every day in your prayer or meditation time, and ask for help to strengthen and direct it for the greatest possible loving and healing effect.

Asking for help strengthens your intent enormously, because others outside the planet's immediate environment rush to amplify the power of your intent. But unless you ask for help they cannot assist you, because you have free will and it is therefore up to you to ask – or not ask! – for help.

What you came to Earth to do requires enormous energy, and that energy is available in abundance, but you must ask for it, and keep asking for it.

Our Divine Destiny

As humans – and as an "aware" human you become a grounding-rod – it is very easy for you to change, redirect, or even stop your intent. To keep it directed requires your focused awareness, which is why you must pray or meditate daily, and also set aside moments during the day to reconfirm your intent.

The disadvantage of the human condition is the ease and flexibility with which you can commit to something, and then forget that commitment or intent. But. . . the great advantage is that once you become aware of this, you can use it to great effect to change anything, and you can direct it powerfully and purposefully in the direction of your choosing.

This flexibility is not available in other realms. So use this ability, direct your intent, hold it firmly, heal your planet, and move all into the new era – the Golden Age of divine abundance and loving harmony, which is the destination that you have all been seeking for so long.

The Golden Age is indeed very close, so just continue to focus your intent, expand your awareness, and bring it to fruition, into blossom, and into your own living experience.

Θ Θ Θ

91   The incredible explosion of healers into Earth's energy fields is no accident

It is indeed good to take a day out from time to time to rest, to relax, and to allow your body to accept and adjust to the new and increased energies flowing through it. These energies will help enormously as you transition into full-conscious awareness, in preparation for the wonderful and dramatic changes that are about to happen in your worldly environment – changes that will literally morph it into the "other-worldly" environment that has been planned and prepared for you for so long.

As you relax, turn inward, and listen to your inner knowing, you will increasingly experience the peace and harmony available to you, as your whole being finally starts coming into perfect balance, allowing you to know exactly what you want and need to do in every moment. The experience, which will become continuous, will bring a happy contentment perman-ently into your lives, as the anxieties and doubts with which you have lived for so long, and to which you are habituated – in fact practically addicted – will just fall away, leaving you wondering if you truly experienced them, or if they were merely a bad dream. And truly that is all they were!

As these new energies continue to flow abundantly into and through you with ever increasing power and efficacy, uplifting all with whom you interact in any way at all, your own awareness of the peace and harmony that surrounds you at all times will increase phenomenally. This will give you greater confidence in your ability to love and accept all unconditionally, and to be a healing-conduit for those with whom you interact, and who are willing and able to accept the energies that flow through you.

This incredible explosion of healers into the Earth's energy fields at this time is no accident, but has long been planned. And now the intent is in effect and sweeping through humanity, the other life forms, and Planet Earth herself in a wonderful acceleration of loving awareness that is raising all rapidly towards full consciousness.

Nothing that you are experiencing or feeling at this time is accidental or coincidental. It is all part of the magnificent, divine plan which, as this stage of it approaches completion, will unite all sentient beings. Permanent, harmonious, and loving cooperation is essential for the ongoing progress of the Creator's eternally evolving and expanding creative endeavor, in which all are united in perfectly focused, loving intent.

What you intend, comes to pass. What all of creation intends explodes into being with a force of power and might that is unimaginable. And only in the state of full consciousness will you be able to withstand the blast of this exquisitely beautiful and loving explosion into new and undreamt-of levels of being.

92 You are never alone in the darkness of your non-awareness

As you follow your chosen path, consciously or in a state of non-awareness, life presents you with choices and opportunities that are created for you – and you alone – because, of course, regardless of your state of awareness, you are the co-creator of your path. How you choose to interact with these opportunities determines which ones you will follow, because the path you have created is extremely well planned, to provides as far as is possible – given that you have freedom of will – an ongoing scenario of comprehensible continuity after each choice that you make.

As you can imagine, this means that the path you have laid out for yourself is hugely complex, with a near-endless selection of options available to you throughout its course. As you progress along it during your human lifetime, making choices in every moment, it becomes increasingly possible for God to intuit the destination for which you are heading – although that can never be absolutely certain due to the consequences of your various changes of mind as you make your way forward. Then, if you are open to suggestion, He can give you a nudge or insight to remind you of your original intent when you co-created your life path with Him prior to your present incarnation.

You can be aware or unaware of the insight, accept it, refuse it, or ignore it; your free will is always yours. But you are never left alone to flounder, lost and confused, in the darkness of your non-awareness. Help is always available, even though you may choose not to believe it or avail of it. And that choice is quite common when you cling tenaciously to your blocks and resistances and stubbornly refuse to open your awareness.

Meditation and relaxation enable you to open into awareness. So make time available for it regularly, and focus on that intent.

ⴱ   ⴱ   ⴱ

93   This grand awakening has been planned for humanity since the dawn of time

At this time, Planet Earth is receiving a large download of spiritual energy, as requested by so many of you in your prayers and meditation, to assist in the spread of awareness that there *is* a spiritual life in which all are involved.

It is quite an awakening for many, who had strongly discounted such a possibility and did not wish to believe in its existence. This is all part of the grand spiritual awakening planned for humanity since the dawn of time. Every day more and more people are receiving the wake-up call to spiritual awareness, and with it comes the often shocking realization that God exists.

As people awaken, they begin to seek guidance – wondering where to look. Many will seek it from established religions, and many more, especially those disenchanted with the established religions, will look elsewhere. Consequently, divine grace is flooding the planet in many different forms, in order that all may find the succor and guidance for which they suddenly find they have a desperate need.

This awakening is leading to a deepening desire on the part of many millions of humans to change forever the way life is lived on Planet Earth. Instead of despairing – as wars of various kinds are fought all over the world, destroying love, hope, lives, and livelihoods – conviction is growing in many hearts that a sea-change in attitudes must and will occur. The need to seek revenge or recompense for personal injury is fading, as people realize that satisfying that need engenders precisely what it is supposed to relieve: further attacks. This is indeed a grand awakening!

The prayers and intentful focus of the newly awakened are very powerful indeed because, on their awakening they are dismayed at the realization of what their attitudes of myopic self-centeredness have wreaked in their lives. They suddenly become aware of their own meanness of spirit and of the effect it has been having on others, before it then rebounds on them.

This sudden awakening releases prodigious amounts of energy that until then had been funneled into emotional attack-and-defense for which it is no longer required. Add to that their intent for change, and for divine assistance in that intent, which releases quantities of additional energy from the divine realms which then vastly increases the efficacy and power of their own newly discovered desires and intents.

Truly great change is occurring right now that will soon usher in the new Golden Age for which all have been longing. Each individual praying, meditating, and intending for it to come into being adds powerfully to the energies already flowing.

Each time you renew your intent, the energies bringing in this divinely ordained change intensify. Keep renewing your intent to bring in the Golden Age – and it will be done.

ɵ   ɵ   ɵ

94   Your places at this heavenly party have been laid and reserved for you

As you wait for the arrival of this magnificent divine event, it is difficult for you not to experience feelings both of great hope and of anxiety and fear of disappointment. You have chosen to be cut off and disconnected from the knowledge available to those in the spiritual realms, so although I give you information with which you resonate intensely, you still lack the sensing of it, the feeling of what is happening. And as the vast majority of humanity is narrowly focused on living physically as humans, without a thought for their spiritual side, let alone awareness of it, it is very difficult to hold the vision of the divine plan on your own.

However, you soon will move into full consciousness. There is absolutely no possibility that this amazing divine event will fail to occur because the Creator's plans are always achieved precisely on schedule. Relax. Let go of your doubts and worries; imagine perfection in every aspect of your existence because that is what you are going to experience. . . eternally.

The divine Consciousness will meld with human consciousness, creating a wonderful awakening for you all. Your places at this heavenly party have been laid and reserved for you, and you will all be there in the magnificence of your true glory.

As this stage of the divine plan approaches completion, the excitement in the spiritual realms is quite palpable. We await your impending arrival into the state of full consciousness with great delight and enthusiasm. The joy when you meet old friends, relatives, guides, angels, and the divine Presence will be supreme.

Deep within yourselves, below your available level of consciousness, you have always had a sense, a knowledge of the big picture of which you are all essential parts, and a knowledge of when you would move from your present state – which you certainly find far less than satisfactory – into your normal and perfect state of utter joy. Yes, of course you have had some happiness in your human lives, but it is as nothing in comparison to what you will soon experience.

Allow yourselves to dream of complete happiness, at Home with your Father in the divine realms – which is where you always are, even though you cannot feel it at present – and prepare for your conscious awareness to awaken into this miraculous, mystical state.

You are divinely loved, divinely respected, and divinely admired for the tremendously difficult paths you have chosen to follow and experience, as you make your way Home through all your Earth lives. We look forward to enjoying with you the most magnificent celebrations.

Ө   Ө   Ө

95   Prayer and meditation are wonderfully visible and apparent to those of us in the spiritual realms

Remember, no one is here by chance; every one of you has a very important task to do – now. Although what you are doing – meditating – may seem to be the same for all of you, it is not. It is only your extremely limited ability to understand the magnificent plan that is in progress which makes it seem that you are all doing the same thing. Each of you – while always being One with the Divine, and therefore with all others – is also a unique individual, doing what you came to do. No one can replace you. Only you can do what you came to do. So please do it, and involve yourself fully and completely in the divine plan, as you promised to do. When all is complete, your joy and delight at what you have achieved will amaze you.

Cut down on the time you spend watching TV, listening to the radio, and reading the various news and gossip publications.

Our Divine Destiny

Allow yourselves time – to spend alone, or with friends, in loving harmonious meditation, which brings immeasurable healing energies to you, which then flow out into your immediate neighborhood, and on from there to mingle and interact most positively and beneficially with similar energies from other individual and group meditation sessions everywhere. Many are now doing this, and the strength and complexity of healing energies being produced is quite phenomenal. Many of you came on Earth to do this, and the interlinking of energies of such a wonderful nature is glorious to behold.

The divine plan in action is truly breathtaking in its scope, and you are all integral, essential parts of it, even though for many of you there is no conscious feedback. In fact, it may seem that your prayers are neither heard nor answered. This is most definitely not the case. What you are achieving is unique – no one but you can do it.

Continue to pray and meditate, with renewed vigor, in any manner that feels comfortable and seems appropriate to you. It is of unquantifiable value, is absolutely essential, and is wonderfully visible and apparent in the spiritual realms where it is harvested, purified, concentrated, and then returned to the planet, where its effects are stunningly successful and effective.

For now, dear Ones, please pray and meditate with your utmost, heartfelt intent, and know that what you are doing is without precedent. There is no alternative available, and because you are doing it so well, no alternative will be required. What you are achieving is fantastic. Keep it going; increase it if you can, and know that all who pray and meditate, wherever and however, of whatever religious persuasion (or none), are saving, preserving, healing, and raising to new levels of spirituality and

176

consciousness this marvelous creation of which we are all most important components.

How you pray or meditate – when or where you do it – does not matter. What matters is to do it with all the energy that is guiding your intent in open and loving cooperation. Be advised that set times when many groups around the world meditate together adds tremendous force and zest to the energies, but see this as an added bonus to the normal individual and group meditations that are constantly in progress all over the planet.

Whenever you pray or meditate, others will also be doing so. Express the intent for those energies to be continuously combined and integrated for greater power and effect. What you awakened ones are doing is marvelous. Know that, and intend that it continue to be so – and it will.

The dawn of this most wonderful age is at hand. Be ready, willing, and able to embrace it with total love and enthusiasm when it arrives!

ϴ   ϴ   ϴ

96   You are here in preparation for this great cosmic event

The Creator's plan for humanity is quite magnificent in its breadth and complexity. It has been in preparation for an extremely long period of time (in your terms) and has no completion or termination point to reach. It always has been and always will be an ongoing, cooperative, creative venture, leading humanity onwards and upwards to ever higher states of spiritual development.

However, the plan does have stages – each one major and of great importance – demonstrating the infinite divine Love that the Creator pours forth in abundance onto all of creation. One of those stages is now approaching completion. And once again the infinite tenderness of divine Love and compassion will pour forth visibly and sensibly for all to experience in wondrous bliss.

You are all here now (and have been many times before) in preparation for this grand cosmic event of which, at a deeper level of yourselves, you truly have much knowledge. The light of grace burns brilliantly just ahead of you, and you will move into it with huge delight to reap the rewards that come with the completion of a major stage in the divine plan.

Your faith has led you forward triumphantly to this point, from which you will all burst forth in an ecstatic explosion of full, blissful, conscious awareness, the like of which has never even been dreamed of. Yes. . . you have held the knowledge of this event deep within yourselves for a very long time. It was promised to you – although the full wonder and meaning of this promise has yet to be disclosed – and the promise itself gave you the strength and the determination in your faith in it to defy all odds, all tribulations, all difficulties – and there have been many – and bring yourselves forward to this point, ready to partake magnificently, joyfully, and with delighted wonder in this gala event.

When a stage like this in the divine plan reaches completion, the joy experienced by all creation is boundless, beyond measure, breathless in its wonder, stunning in its magnificence. You have all essentially arrived for the party; the lights are out, and all is dark; the anticipation is exquisite and intense, almost uncontainable; and the lights are about to be switched on!

You have absolutely no idea how fabulous it is about to become — any moment now. Hang in there! You have the strength and the assistance to enable you to do so. The waiting is inconsequential when compared to the rewards to come.

Θ   Θ   Θ

97   Life's trials and tribulations are almost over

The abundant and fruitful harvest for which you have all been waiting is truly at hand. Your patience has been exemplary – indeed, astonishing! – and is to be most generously rewarded as the divine plan reaches its next stage of completion.

The divine plan for creation is, of course, eternally evolving and developing, and will never reach completion in your sense of the word, because it is an eternally ongoing, creative expression of divine Love that becomes ever more fulfilling as it eternally unfolds. However, it does have stages which can be identified in your terms, and it is one of these that is approaching abundant fruition at this time. And soon that will be readily and wonderfully apparent to you, and to all the sentient beings in your exceptionally diverse environment.

As you wait for the last few details to fall into place – allowing all to move forward again with (in your terms) incredible speed – prepare to be uplifted in amazement and wonder, delight and unimaginable joy. The Creator's Desire and Intent for you all to experience infinite happiness and bliss will not be restrained or prevented, but will burst forth into your living experience with a power and majesty that will leave you stunned with joy, and blissful beyond the bounds of your ability to imagine.

Relax, meditate, and relish the experience of these last few moments of what is basically the total sensory deprivation in which you have been living for as long as you can remember. It is such a contrast to the Reality into which you are about to re-awaken.

All is going forward very smoothly, just as planned, without let or hindrance. Soon, as all becomes abundantly clear to you – when you all enter into full consciousness and total awareness – a supreme sense of peace and love will envelop you, and you will realize that at last you have come Home.

And what a homecoming it will be, as all those whom you have ever known and loved since before time began turn out to greet you at the gala reception our Creator has prepared for you. You will be overwhelmed, overjoyed, and (in your colloquial way of saying things) "over the moon" with delight, laughter, and happiness. It is an event that we in the spiritual realms are greatly looking forward to, and which we are already reveling in, as it truly is already happening – you just are not yet aware of it.

Life's trials and tribulations, which you have so willingly endured, are almost over. And we look forward with great, loving anticipation to the joyful amazement that we shall see you experience, as you discover and realize the wonder of the reward that has been so lovingly prepared for you all.

Our hearts are filled to bursting with love for you, and we look forward to the absolute bliss you are soon to experience. Happiness and delight, joy and laughter infinitely beyond your wildest dreams are available for the asking. And you will ask, knowing with complete confidence that they will be delivered. And our delight as you "unwrap your packages" will equal yours.

Θ   Θ   Θ

98 The seductions of the human condition distract you from the wonderful gift of awareness

The life plans upon which entities embark, when they choose to experience life as humans on Planet Earth, are quite remarkable in their planning and execution. To plan a human existence with the help of your guides, and to have it accepted by God as viable, is a very great undertaking. You have no idea how much thought and preparation are involved in the planning stage. A great number of options are built into the planned life path in order to allow for as many variations as can reasonably be expected to occur during an earthly existence, but without so distracting the soul that it completely loses its way.

Once the soul arrives on Earth, the possible and probable experiences and opportunities available to it are multitudinous, and to formulate a plan in advance that is flexible enough to allow the soul to cope with every situation in a way that provides continuing spiritual growth is creatively very demanding.

During Earth life, the intended lessons always occur, even though their meaning and their value may not be noticed or understood until well after the human death experience. After death, there is much pondering and contemplation in order to take every advantage of the now fully-remembered life experience in all its myriad details. This allows the lessons to be fully understood, and the wisdom obtained from that understanding to be assimilated into the entity's conscious awareness. Once that happens, the information and wisdom obtained is always instantly available to it. So you can appreciate that a soul accumulates a vast storehouse of knowledge and wisdom over the eons that it incarnates on Earth for a series of human lives.

Each time it partakes of human existence, it separates itself

181

from this storehouse – this fount of wisdom – in order to obtain the greatest possible learning experience while on Earth. Nevertheless, it maintains contact with its intuition so that it is never without guidance of the highest order, unless it allows itself to be distracted or chooses to switch off its awareness.

Awareness is always there for souls experiencing a human existence; they have only to allow it in. But frequently the seductions and attractions of the human condition distract them from it, or encourage them to ignore this marvelous gift. And sometimes they choose to experience selective awareness which they think gives them power (and in human terms it seems to do so). Often they believe – but for a limited time only – that the end justifies the means, and that path of course leads eventually to grief and sorrow, and is therefore a most powerful learning experience.

Just remember that every path is valid, and leads always to greater love and wisdom. To judge is to distract yourselves from your own paths, thus delaying your inevitable union with your divine Father. Stick with your own path. Find out who you are. Then be that at all times.

Θ Θ Θ

99 Power provides a great challenge to the love that humans exemplify

Human life is meant to be an ongoing stream of experiences and opportunities that enable great strides to be made in personal spiritual growth. It is for this reason that entities choose to incarnate as humans. The human environment has been most carefully planned by the Creator – in cooperation and agreement with those who choose to experience human existence – to provide an enormous selection of difficult and demanding scenarios, of rewarding and challenging experiences in an extremely condensed form, so that spiritual progress can be made very rapidly indeed, allowing the entity to return home in record time.

The downside is the possibility – also frequently experienced – of entering a repetitious cycle of incarnations where the wisdom and growth gained in one cycle is apparently lost and discarded in the next, when it is used inappropriately in a quest for power. Then the lesson has to be relearned.

The power of seduction and the seduction of power are very strong and distracting energies in this environment. This is often not recognized until a considerable number of incarnations have occurred, although each human has all the necessary information and intuitive knowing to realize this in every moment of his existence. Power is extremely alluring, and this is one of the main reasons why entities choose to become human. It provides such a great challenge to the love and the wisdom that they exemplify and, therefore, such satisfaction when they complete the cycle.

Life's purpose is growth and expansion, lovingly created for the infinite glory of the divine Being, which is everything ever created. Absolutely everything – from the smallest particle to the largest universe – exists in order to grow in love, wisdom, and knowledge. It is unending. . . and magnificent.

The smallest particles of which your scientists are aware are far larger than the smallest particles that exist; and the largest galaxies of which astronomers are aware are far smaller than the largest galaxies that exist. Humanity's ability to see and calculate is truly very limited, even though it appears that you have seen and understood so much. When the true Reality of divine creation becomes apparent to you, it will be stunningly magnificent, brilliant, colorful, musical, sensual, scented, textured – completely wondrous. So far, the most mystical among you have had only the slightest glimpse of the infinite delights of the Divine.

ϴ   ϴ   ϴ

100   It is the divine Will that pain and fear should cease – permanently

Humanity has experienced much pain and suffering over the eons, and it seems to be unending. However, this is to change. There has been more than enough fear, anxiety, and disappointment, and it is the divine Will that it shall cease. . . permanently!

God has never required humanity to suffer, and He has never judged or punished you. But free will has given you enormous power which you have found most seductive, and which you have frequently used most unwisely. The time for that kind of behavior and that kind of deeply painful experience – brought about because you are free. . . free to damage, free to destroy, free to corrupt, free to inflict pain – is at an end. You have had more than enough of it, and a large majority of you want to bring it to an end. . . and so you shall. You are ready – after eons of self-inflicted pain, disillusionment, and disappointment – to release those experiences from your reality permanently. Humanity has decided to live in peace, harmony, wisdom, and love; that is also the Creator's divine Will. It is what you have all been working towards, even though it is less than totally apparent in your limited human environment.

God loves His divine creation with an infinite passion, as a father loves his children. He has given you free will and the ability to use it. It is your choice whether to use it cooperatively or competitively, and over the last two or three decades you have moved inexorably towards harmony and cooperation.

The time is approaching very rapidly for that harmonious, cooperative human intent to be fully realized. Full consciousness, delight, joy, and harmony will be the result of that intent. Your trials and tribulations are very nearly over, and soon you will move into that state, which your divine Father has always wanted you to enjoy.

His delight in preparing it for you and in seeing you accept and enjoy it is completely beyond description. He wants only for you to be infinitely happy and joyful, and when you are ready to accept that momentous divine gift it will be given to you.

You are very nearly ready, so you can soon expect to move into that supreme state. Open your hearts in preparation for this magnificent divine gift – and it will become yours to experience eternally.

The Creator's Love for you all is vast, quite beyond the bounds of your ability to imagine. So relax. . . and allow it to permeate and suffuse you utterly. There will be absolutely no disappointments, no judgments, and no punishments, only perfect joy – because God is infinite Love, and that is what He has prepared for you: joy beyond your ability as humans to imagine. Nor is there any need to attempt to imagine that state, because shortly you will be experiencing it.

Infinite joy and bliss are about to be your normal state of existence.

Ɵ   Ɵ   Ɵ

101 Acceptance of yourself allows your true desire to be strongly sensed

As you are well aware, your life on Planet Earth is a wonderful opportunity for great spiritual growth and development. You chose to be on Earth because of the tremendous potential for growth that the human experience provides. Once you incarnated, the vision you had before birth of your earthly life was buried deep within you and seems to be inaccessible. This is why many humans lose sight of or forget the intention and the life plan with which they arrived.

Much time is spent wondering, "What is it all about?" and the various religions that are supposed to help you work this out frequently bury you in wholly inappropriate dogma, platitudes, and rules which severely limit and impede you as you try to find your own personal path.

For growth to occur, a loving and open heart is essential, and regular meditation, reflection, and time given solely to yourself will lead you towards the light (that personal sense of inner knowing), and towards your own personal path of truth and integrity.

The demands of society often cloud your ability to recognize your path, and encourage you to seek your own by following someone else's! Acceptance of yourself and especially of your confusion about who you are and what you are supposed to be doing with your life greatly assists you in the necessary opening of your heart. This allows your vision, your true desire, and the intent with which you incarnated to be strongly sensed, so that you begin to know more and more surely whether or not you are living the life that you intended. The more you feel this with your inner knowing, the more it will just happen for you.

(The demands to which I referred are the dogmatic and supposedly incontrovertible beliefs of a race, culture, or religion that are judgmental and unaccepting of other points of view. What a recipe for disharmony, discontent, anger, and confusion they have been!)

Humanity is here to wake up and grow. And yet many of you strongly resist doing so, which takes up an inordinate amount of your energy. Sit back and open your perception; listen to your inner promptings, and you will find yourselves filled with an abundance of energy that encourages you to follow them. You will begin to see clearly what it is that you do want to do, enabling you to override your fears and anxieties.

Everything you need is within you. So spend time – plenty of time (and you do have all you need) – in reflection and meditation, to allow the knowledge and wisdom you need to flow abundantly into your awareness, offering you the most appropriate and self-authenticated guidance in every moment.

Relax. . . open up. . . allow. And then accept the Creator's most wonderful gift to you – Life! Then live it, and enjoy it. It truly is very simple, although not always easy. So do not try to complicate it!

Θ   Θ   Θ

102   All will become instantly aware that they always knew this was what was planned

The divine plan is rolling along rapidly and perfectly, as it does in every moment. When the time for the great event arrives, humanity will see and become aware of what has been going on for so many eons, as it bursts into full consciousness like buds bursting into flower, as this stage of the divine plan is completed and the Golden Age of love, harmony, and peace arrives.

You are almost ready now for this magnificent occasion which will be with you very shortly, delighting you in ways that you could never have imagined. The remaining preparations are being completed so that soon all will be revealed as our divine Creator intends. Your times of waiting, of wondering, of hoping, of skepticism, and in some cases of total disbelief are practically over. At the moment of change – as all come together in peace and harmonious cooperation – all your fears, worries, and mistrust will be swept away as all become instantly aware that they always knew that this was what was planned. They will remember with great joy and satisfaction why they chose to be human at this point in the divine plan.

Very soon now all will come to fruition, bringing you the rewards for which you have been yearning and working towards for so long. Those few who choose not to participate will not find themselves abandoned, discarded, or inhabiting an environment that in any way resembles what humans have imagined hell, purgatory, or limbo to be. They will in fact continue to live in the environment to which they have become accustomed. But their memories of those with whom they normally interact – who have chosen full consciousness and a magnificent divine home-coming – will just evaporate, so that everything will appear quite normal to them. When they are ready to advance once more on their spiritual journeys, abundant divine assistance will be available, as it always has been, to help them on their way.

For the majority of you who will move instantly home to full consciousness, that moment will occur most propitiously, exactly as divinely determined, with smoothness and precision. There will be absolutely no conflicts or disasters at the moment of transformation, caused, for example, by vehicles going out of control. All will move at their own personal appropriate moment into full consciousness without in any manner affecting the movement of anyone else.

Suddenly, you will be fully conscious, completely present, and in the spot that you have chosen to be in to experience this wonderful event. You will be surrounded by the closest members of your divine, spiritual family, enveloped in joy and harmony, and with full knowledge of your divine destiny. It will be a moment of supreme happiness and satisfaction, forever increasing in intensity at exactly the pace that you desire, so that your contentment will be utterly perfect.

You truly will be in that state in a very short time, and deep within yourselves you know it! Let that knowledge rise to the surface of your human awareness, and enjoy fully the brief period remaining in your present three-dimensional reality.

Θ   Θ   Θ

103   The preparations have led inevitably to this time of fruition

Life for all of you on Earth is changing dramatically. You know it, you sense it, and it is happening – right now. You came to Earth to help prepare for these changes and then put them into effect. The harvest time has arrived; the preparations have led inevitably to this time of fruition. The work that you have been doing constantly in other realms – the divine spiritual realms – is now bearing divine fruit.

You, all humans, have always known that this time would come. God could have created this moment – this point of completion – eons ago. But it would have meant overriding your free will and taking from you the delight and satisfaction that you will experience when you realize what your earthly lives have achieved.

To give you an analogy – one that is totally inadequate, but which gives you a hint of understanding, a tiny handle on an enormous divine mystery: it would have been rather like parents not allowing their infant to crawl, then walk, then run, but always carrying it. Yes, it might well be basically contented but it would miss out on the joy and fulfillment of doing things for itself, and playing the games that are only possible for one who is personally mobile.

And so you have crawled and walked and run, and now you are ready to fly! To bi-locate! To be, for example, anywhere you wish to be – instantly! You cannot imagine – even in your wildest dreams – the joys that are about to become permanent features of your lives. Sorrow, anxiety, fear, disappointment, banality, tedium, and boredom are experiences of the past – to be released, forever.

190

Those travails can now cease; there is no longer any need for them because the time for humanity's release from the illusion is at hand. Open your hearts, accept and allow the divine energy to permeate you completely, filling you with the bliss, wonder, and happiness for which you have been preparing for so long.

It is here for you now – in this very moment. Allow yourselves to accept this divine gift which is your rightful inheritance. Immerse yourselves in the divine grace, the divine bliss, the divine joy that the Creator has prepared for you. You need only say, "Yes, I accept!" And it is yours – now!

Ө   Ө   Ө

104   As we achieve a preordained level within creation, we move swiftly and suddenly up to the next level

As the divine plan for Planet Earth, and the life forms she supports, continues to unfold so lovingly and successfully, more and more of humanity is beginning to realize that something is going on: there is a feeling of change in the air, and a sense of hopeful anticipation.

People are beginning to look at their personal relationships in a new and in fact truly wondrous way and are starting to see what marvelous improvements can be made to them when they cooperate harmoniously with one another other so that all may benefit. It is happening on a small scale at present, but the effect is already enormous and powerful, continually doubling and redoubling, so that soon very few people will be left unaware of this new sense of hope that "anything is possible," and that life can be a truly uplifting experience.

And as this new and, for many, unaccustomed sense of well-being starts to seep into their conscious awareness, they will come to the realization that there is indeed a divine Intelligence directing all of creation. They will realize that they – every single one of them – have a direct connection to this divine Being, and that all they have to do is to relax into it and allow the amazing energies available from it to suffuse them. It will be as though they were soaking in a tub of the most incredibly soothing liquid of acceptance and Love, at just the right temperature for each individual's metabolism, so that they feel wholly at one with, united with, and in fact a part of the liquid within which they are basking in such divine contentment. The divine plan is of course absolutely on schedule; it always has been, and it always will be. The Creator is perfect and so is His planning. However, your ability to understand and interpret its meaning for you frequently leaves much to be desired.

We – all of God's created conscious entities – are on a continuing path of spiritual growth and development, and we always will be, as we progress towards the perfection that He demonstrates for us continuously.

The individual paths that each of us has chosen to follow – and there are billions and billions of us throughout the vastness of creation – sometimes harmonize most beautifully together, and sometimes seem to be totally at odds with, in opposition to, or even at war with each other. And yet, although often extremely difficult if not impossible for us to understand, they are directing us continuously towards perfect, divine harmony.

When those who are consciously attempting to live their lives in harmony with the Divine come into contact with others of the same intent who are coming from a different direction or perception, the short term results can appear to you to be somewhat at odds, rather like two (or more) jugglers juggling many balls as they stand side by side. Invariably at some point they will interfere with each other and all the balls fall. But, even as they fall the jugglers perceive the possibility of harmoniously integrating their acts so that they can juggle together, producing a much more entrancing display. And so they agree to work together to accomplish this.

Life is like this to a certain extent, which is why it is experienced as having ups and downs, good times and bad times, exciting times and boring times, happy times and sad times, loving times and hating times, peaceful times and chaotic times. It is all part of the divine plan that constantly assists and guides us along our individual paths towards harmonious integration and spiritual union.

As we achieve a certain preordained level of integration and accord within creation, we move swiftly and suddenly up to the next level, creating new wonder and delight in our lives, and increasing our motivation to grow and develop further. Sometimes we appear to take a great spiritual tumble into a lower stage of development, which is hellish, depressing, and seemingly hopeless. And yet this is something that, in consultation with the Creator, our guides, and our higher Self, we have decided to experience for the great benefits – wholly inconceivable to us during the time span of the experience – and insights that will result from it and that will culminate in unimaginable joy.

⊖   ⊖   ⊖

105   Your reason for being will become wonderfully clear to you

As you know, much is changing in your environment at the moment, and these changes are being very deeply felt and experienced by all forms of life on the dearly loved planet you know as Earth. These changes were planned a very long time ago by the Creator – in His Wisdom and Love – to create an environment suitable to the fully developed spiritual beings that you are about to become. The changes are of an enormous magnitude, leading onwards and upwards to full awareness of your unity with the Creator – at all times – constantly – in every moment. You will be able to see, experience, and understand your creative powers, and how you have been using them constantly since you were first created, and how you will continue to use them in joy and love with the complete confidence of being One in and with the Creator. Your sense of purpose, your reason for being, will become abundantly and wonderfully clear to you as you bask in the glory of the Divine.

All is going absolutely as planned and intended by the divine Being. And all who are One in unity with Him are creating an environment that becomes increasingly beautiful and pleasing to Him. The setbacks, disasters, and catastrophes that you experience in your three-dimensional reality are brilliant in design when seen – as you will soon again see everything – in the overall context of the vast and wondrous creation that is All That Is.

Your faith and patience has in truth been, and continues to be, wondrous to behold from the elevated spiritual vantage point from which those in our realm (the realm in which you will soon rejoin us) observe your illusory reality.

It is like a magnificent theatrical production, which is about to come to its conclusion to the thunderous applause of us, the audience, who will bombard you with flowers and cheers as we give you a well-deserved standing ovation for the magnificent performance to which you have treated us.

Hang in there. . . . Your aches and pains, your fears, doubts, and anxieties will soon dissipate like morning mist.

Ө   Ө   Ө

106   All will return to the One when they are ready

The Earth changes that are occurring now, and that are planned for the immediate future, are of a momentous nature, and most of humanity will be amazed and astonished when they become aware of what is happening to their beloved planet and to all of the life systems that she has been supporting so hospitably for so long.

The surprise will change to wonder as the full implications of what is happening becomes generally known and understood by those who choose to be aware. There are indeed many who still resist the loving energies of change and growth that are pouring down to awaken humanity's spirituality, and to envelop each soul in a rapture of happiness and bliss. If they continue to resist and refuse to awaken into the new Golden Age that has been prepared for them, they will be free to move (and greatly assisted in that choice) to an environment with which they can resonate more comfortably.

No one will be punished or discarded, and you should not judge or condemn those who choose not to partake in the new reality of abundance and love. Each has free will and the absolute right to move at his own pace along the homeward path to unity with the Divine. To attempt to force the pace of those who wish to travel more slowly would be a violation of their God-given rights, and would demonstrate a sorry lack of integrity and wisdom. All are "saved"; and all will return to the One when they are ready. And they will then be welcomed with the greatest of joy and love.

The enlightened among you, who are choosing to move forward at this time, need not concern yourselves with those who choose a different "reality" even if they are at present closely and intimately involved in your life. You will soon understand how beautifully the divine plan has been constructed, allowing for no disappointments or broken promises.

On the deepest levels, everything – absolutely everything – is on target and on schedule. And for those who choose to participate (and for many who to you do not appear to be ready but who will indeed awaken in good time to do so), complete bliss and ecstasy will shortly envelop you as the grand celebrations commence.

Your reward is abundantly at hand. Your tremendous faith and devotion have brought you successfully to the threshold of this abundant, new and Golden Age. . . . And you are about to enter.

Θ   Θ   Θ

107   It is important to understand your reasons for being on Planet Earth at this point

As humanity awaits the unfolding of the Creator's divine plan, it is a good time for all to reflect, meditate, and pray for guidance concerning their life's purpose and intent. It is important to understand your reasons for being present in physical form on Planet Earth at this point on her evolutionary path. A lot is demanded of you, and you are all capable of rising to these demands. But you really do need to get fully in touch with your inner, God-given knowing, so that you can take appropriate action, or relax in appropriate inaction as the situation demands.

Ask your guides, your full Self, and the Creator Himself to assist and energize your individual inner search to find, identify, and release the blocks – psychic, physical, mental, and emotional – that you all have. They interfere with your chosen task of co-creating with each other, with all of created consciousness, with the Creator Himself, and in accordance with the divine plan that He is bringing to glorious and abundant fruition at this time.

You have all chosen to be here, fully using your own amazing energies to bring forth this awesome, beautiful, and powerful event which will change forever, and most gloriously, the way consciousness experiences itself, and the Divine.

It is essential for you to make the full one hundred percent of your power and energy available for this task. And in order to do this, all your blocks, blind spots, denials, and negations must be released so that your energies may flow with total freedom, unencumbered by the many uncommitted, confused, and mis-directed energies that have been stored within almost all of you in great profusion.

Now is the time to address and release these blocks. The need is urgent; so make your intent to do so very clear when you meditate (and you must meditate), when you awaken, and before going to sleep. And during the day, recall your intent fre-quently. The more conscious you allow yourself to be of this intent – which is of course a very major part of your reason for experiencing physical reality – the more we on the higher realms can assist you.

You are doing it, each of you, for yourself and also for all of creation. It is an enormously demanding task of the utmost importance, and you need absolutely all the assistance that it is possible for you to receive. Keep strengthening your intent. Keep bringing it into your conscious awareness, to allow the events the Creator has planned for all to come to fruition – rapidly, elegantly, beautifully, and perfectly – for His total joy and bliss, and the total joy and bliss of all those whom He has in His beneficent Love and Wisdom created.

Relax and allow all the distractions and energy drains – onto which you are holding so strongly – to just melt away in divine Love. This is an urgent need at this time. So do it. . . now. And be conscious and alert. And intend with all your heart, so that we too can assist in raising all of consciousness to the level that He has always intended that it should attain. You will be carrying and caring for many who had intended to participate – but who have forgotten their intent and have misplaced their awareness. But we can and will do it, because that is the Creator's Intent, and it will not be prevented.

This is a time of great joy as you allow yourselves to participate fully and completely.

Ө   Ө   Ө

108   The more clearly you can define your need, the more we can assist you

When you ask for help – in prayer or meditation, when relaxing, or when you feel an immediate need for it – it increases the effectiveness of your request if you make it a short concentrated attempt to focus very precisely on what it is you need help with. The more clearly you can define your need – and it only has to be done briefly – the more effectively we, your loving guides and friends, can assist you. A brief, very focused intent on precisely what you need will work wonders.

Your life is yours to live any way you choose to; and you decide in every moment, whether you want to be aware of that or not. All That Is, the saints, angels, guides, and your full Self are all available, instantly and always, to help you to observe, to see, to understand, to become enlightened, and to move into the Light. They want to help you, they want to see you happy and contented, but you have to want that too. And you have to ask for their help. And because to be truly human you have to live in the now moment, because that is when life *is*, you have to make it your intent in every moment to seek help from all those many willing and able helpers, and to accept it when it is given.

It really is incredibly easy; just allow all those who agreed before you incarnated to be at your side whenever you needed them to assist you. You do not need to do anything alone because there are many loving entities longing to help you in the most appropriate way possible, in every moment of your life. You only have to ask, and then accept what is offered. Open your heart, be aware, allow. You can do nothing on your own because you never are alone, as you are forever One with the Divine.

Separation is an illusion. Keep reminding yourself of this, and slowly the illusion will fade, and once again you will experience unity, oneness, and the joy and bliss that are forever present in that glorious state.

Relaxation and meditation, quiet withdrawal from the hustle and bustle and the incredible noise and distraction of your three-dimensional, security-seeking existence are what is required. Ask for help to still your mind – and truly intend it – and you will achieve that beautiful state of peace in which your worries and anxieties shrink almost into insignificance, and you become truly aware that you can indeed, with all the wonderful help and guidance you are receiving, solve every problem that you need to solve, and happily allow any other problems to resolve themselves – as they most certainly will.

Life will indeed flow for you, beautifully, once you allow it to, instead of trying to dam it and control it, which truly is an incredible waste of time and effort that could be used so efficaciously elsewhere.

Θ   Θ   Θ

109   Disasters are just sudden changes of direction

All is well – as deep within yourself you are truly aware. Outward appearances of confusion, chaos, and disaster in your life are simply signs, notices, and attention-grabbers reminding you that you are being distracted from your life's purpose and need to get back to it. When you follow your path to fulfill your life's purpose, you realize that there truly is no confusion and no chaos, because everything has a divine purpose that is always wholly appropriate.

Disasters are just sudden (and in human terms) unexpected changes of direction. They always lead towards greater insight, knowledge, and wisdom. Some people – maybe many – choose not to see this. But if you look back, you will see that there have always been benefits that have emerged from disasters. Disasters are hardly ever what they seem. You can always make tremendous spurts of growth from the apparent chaos that a disaster brings about.

Everything grows originally out of chaos, so it is not something to be avoided, but rather to be welcomed as it always leads forward. In your own lives, you have all, many times, experienced situations that at the time were most unwelcome, and yet, if you are truly honest with yourself, you must admit that what actually developed from those conditions was very beneficial.

110   Stand back and observe what is going on

As you are well aware, life's trials and tribulations are experiences that you have chosen, to assist you with your spiritual growth, and so are the joys and successes. They come rolling along to meet you, just as planned, and if you have been developing as planned, you cope with them admirably. If, however, you have taken some "wrong" turnings and find yourself "stuck," the challenges of life may appear unmanageable and lead you to see yourself as a hapless victim of circumstances, of the power and manipulation of others, or of God.

This is of course ridiculous! When you planned your life, you were very aware that it would be a life of spiritual blindness, deafness, amnesia, and unawareness, and you factored in allowances for this in your plan. You came in with an abundance of those talents and abilities required to follow and complete your chosen path. A failure to take advantage of the appropriate options available to you is not in the long run a failure, because you learn enormously on a spiritual level from the apparent set-backs that you experience during your human existence.

Nevertheless, you do most certainly have the ability to move out from under this inappropriate mountain of burdensome experiences any time you so desire. It is purely a question of giving yourself time, and refusing to allow yourself to be rushed and pressured by the circumstances in which you find yourself so unpleasantly enmeshed. Therefore, stand back! Observe what is going on, and take time to look around. Really take your time as there is a lot to see, understand, and come to terms with.

Basically, you have set yourself up – and this is very tough to admit and accept. You have pride; you have a logical mind; you are not enjoying the experiences; and logically, why would you set yourself up so unpleasantly? "Ridiculous!" you tell yourself. "There must be some other powers or energies doing this to me."

But there really are no "others" out there making your life a misery, because they are all far too busy making their own lives a misery! How often do you wonder and worry about how others see you, and whether they really understand you and appreciate how hard you are trying? With all this going on, you do not have time to concern yourself with interfering in other people's lives. And other people are in the same boat. With all their own inappropriate concerns and worries, they too have no time to spend trying to make your life a misery. It may seem that that is what they are trying to do, but what they are doing, which you think is directed at you, are merely responses to their own concerns and worries.

Once you understand and accept this, you can easily give yourself the time to sit back and observe. Then, comprehension that you are not helpless will enable you to live your life, instead of preventing life with your unfounded fears and anxieties.

111 Move with change to create something you desire

Creation is a continuous, ongoing event that expresses itself in an infinite number of ways that change in every moment. Nothing is static. Stasis would be a cessation of the divine creative force. . . and that just is not possible. Consequently, all is constantly in a state of change or flux.

All that can be constant is change itself. And yet humanity frequently tries to prevent change, to cause stasis, instead of moving with change and into change, to create something it desires.

When change is resisted, conflict ensues between the intent, which is then concealed and denied, and the outcome, which is often unexpected and perhaps shocking – because of the denial and refusal to be aware of the intent.

As long as you blind yourselves to your true intent, and as long as you hide your intent under a deluge of denial and repression, you will be surprised and shocked by the results your intent achieves. As long as you choose to hide your intent from your conscious awareness, you will remain unable to alter your intent, and unable to create experiences that will please and delight you.

It is akin to being in a state of civil war with yourself: the right hand remaining unaware and unadvised of the what the left is doing. And so your "intent" seems to sabotage your "intent." If this is how you are experiencing your life, you are getting a very clear wake-up call – a call to become aware, to listen to your inner knowing, which will enable you to change your intent so that you experience life as satisfying, fulfilling, and a delight.

Everything you experience is chosen by you to guide you into awareness, into full consciousness, back to your Source, All That Is. The more extreme your experiences, the more loudly and vociferously your true Self is trying to attract your attention

So, pay attention. . . . It will lead you to joy!

Θ   Θ   Θ

112   All started in unity

Live in the moment. . . always. . . enjoying your continuing journey of self-discovery, which, to put it in physical terms if you wish to imagine it that way, would be like finding your dream site, building your dream house, and continually developing the house and the environment in which you have placed it, furnishing and decorating it beautifully. Always it would be beautiful, from the initial discovery of the site, the planning and designing of the building, the laying of the first brick, the hanging of the first picture, and endlessly on, never looking to finish, but only to continue adding and developing and expanding the beauty of your creation.

That is what the unending journey is all about: creating and experiencing your beautiful self in ever more wonderful and satisfying ways. You have no time for disappointments, dissatisfactions, or regrets; you are too busy journeying forward, continuously creating the beauty, joy, and bliss that you intend to experience. The journey is endless, endlessly fulfilling, and that is the way you want it. So live it, experience it, enjoy it, and you will be eternally fulfilled.

Life is a series of experiences that an individual chooses to undergo in order to advance her spiritual development as she works her way back along her path to union with the Creator.

All started in unity. Then, in order to expand and develop the creative power of the Divine, all separated into individuality so that each might experience in their own way what it is to create. Some create abundance, others poverty; some create power, others powerlessness. But each creates and experiences what she chooses. Nothing is imposed from without; all is created from within. When one who has chosen to experience victimization has had enough, all she has to do is to move on. Nothing holds her there except her own intent.

Everyone has intent, though many choose to hide their intent from themselves. And so they are able to blind themselves to the fact that they have chosen to be victims, manipulators, or enablers. To escape from this self-imposed trap, it is essential to take time alone with the mind quietened, so that the true Self can be heard and sensed, putting one in contact with one's inner knowing, and preparing oneself for changes in the way one chooses to experience life.

Ѳ   Ѳ   Ѳ

113   Do what you want to do, because that is to follow your path

Life's ups and downs are quite natural, and there is no need to concern yourself with them unduly. Do what you want to do, and allow life to flow as it will. This will attune you to the energy vibrations with which you resonate most comfortably. When you do this, the ups and downs will feel less abrupt. Life flow and swirls, and the eddies and powerful currents this creates provide a vastly varied pattern of opportunities from which an individual can choose a selection that is best suited to her own growth.

Everyone's needs are different, and so every path is different. And even when people live through identical events, they experience them in their own unique way. Another's path or experience can never be yours, even though it may be incredibly similar. Surviving a fire, downhill skiing, or eating ice cream are experiences that can be imagined. And so you can empathize with another's experience, but you cannot live it, because your experience is yours and hers is hers. You can imagine what it feels like; but she feels it.

The currents of life can carry you forward at quite a pace, apparently causing great progress in your development, then sweep you into a backwater where it seems you are stagnating. . . achieving nothing. But that is not how spiritual growth goes. The apparent rush of achievement is of no greater value than the apparent emptiness or lack of growth you experience in the periods of stillness or apparent stagnation. All are equally necessary and valid steps on your path; all of them are required for your full development, and, if missed out, will have to be accomplished later, which can lead to a lot of anxious soul-searching.

It can feel a lot easier to go with the flow. But even if you always struggle against it, you will eventually get there – which is of course right here, where you are now! So do what you want to do, because that is to follow your path. Don't bother to compare it to another's, as each person's is unique.

Life has many delightful surprises in store for those who can live in open awareness. Joy will flow in at the most unexpected moments as they float along on the currents of life, breathing in all it has to offer, and becoming fully alive in the process. Whatever you do or perceive moves you further along the path of your spiritual growth in an effortless expansion of conscious awareness, for there is no limit to the possibilities for growth. Life will expand constantly if you allow it to, taking you on a ceaseless journey of exploration and discovery.

The journey is the reason for existence; there is no destination, and there is no starting place, so chasing results is distracting and self-defeating. It is, of course, quite unlike a physical journey, and that causes much confusion because many people think of this journey in terms of going home. . . when they are in fact already Home. The journey *is* Home because that is where you are at all times, even though you may be – and probably are – unaware of it.

ϴ   ϴ   ϴ

114   "Thy Will be done"

As you wait, much is happening to finalize the preparations for humanity's move into full consciousness. Your prayers, relaxation, and meditation are most important, so do not neglect them. As you wait, be aware that all of us in the spiritual realms are also very involved in bringing this magnificent event to fruition. All have their part to play.

Very soon now, all will be fully conscious. Have no doubts, because you are very close to the moment of change. We can feel its approach and are in a state of most eager anticipation. Fun, delight, and joy will envelop you, as life as you know and experience it at present changes direction to bring you into full consciousness.

Understanding, harmony, peace, and love will pour into your awareness as you watch the unfolding of the Creator's divine plan into its next stage. Your happiness will be complete as you recognize and experience your unbreakable connection to the divine One, God, our heavenly Father.

As you wait, accept. . . . Accept His creation as you presently experience it as humans on Planet Earth. Release all judgment, of others, of the planet, and of God. Trust His divine Intention and join with Him in making the intention: "Thy Will be done." It is a very powerful and stabilizing prayer, which is always needed, and particularly at the moment of change, which is approaching very rapidly.

Accept and acknowledge everything you are feeling and experiencing – without judgment, without fear or anxiety, and allow yourself. . . yes, *allow* yourself to accept full consciousness instantly and wholeheartedly at the moment of change. In so doing, you will move into that new divine state of being with skill and competence, ready to continue on your newly defined path, which will be instantly recognizable.

Suddenly, as all becomes clear, you will find yourself doing in every moment precisely what is divinely appropriate, with great joy and ease, as you meet, mix, and mingle with all the old friends and relatives whom you have always loved, and from whom you have apparently been separated for so long.

As I have so often told you before, it will be time of utmost joy, and it is almost upon you. The waiting time is practically over, and soon all will be revealed as the great divine event awakens you into full and wonderful consciousness of God's plan for His creation, overwhelming you with delight.

ϴ   ϴ   ϴ

115   Being human is like living in a tightly insulated house

The divine plan is flowing smoothly, just as the Creator intends; and is perfectly on schedule, just as He intends. Very soon you will all be fully aware of your nature as part of the Divine.

It is difficult for you to believe this because, as humans, you are intensely aware of what humanity is doing all around you, and that is where you place almost all your focus. As humans, focusing on the spiritual is very difficult, which is why all spiritual guides and mentors encourage you to clear your mind of thoughts by meditating. This opens up your spiritual awareness and helps you to get in touch with your intuition and with the immense fields of knowledge that are available in the spiritual realms.

Being human is a bit like living in a tightly insulated house: nothing from the vast outdoors can enter, and therefore you have no knowledge of it. But if you open a window just a crack, some outside air seeps in. When you meditate and go more deeply into the meditative state, it is as though you went through the house opening the windows and doors, and allowing the fresh air to flow in. So, to practice your meditation regularly and frequently is most important for your spiritual development as it helps prepare you for the fully-conscious state into which you will all be moving.

Full consciousness is a truly divine state, and quite wondrous to experience. You are, each individual, rather like a drop of water in the ocean, aware that you are but a single drop. At the same time you are aware of and are experiencing everything that the ocean experiences, which is an indescribably happy and joyful feeling. However, even this is a hopelessly inadequate analogy with which to attempt to describe the joy and bliss that full consciousness will bring you.

Before long, you will be fully conscious, and your joy and happiness will be complete, absolute, eternal, infinite. And if you cannot truly believe that right now, do not worry. Full consciousness will very shortly envelop you, as God has promised.

So while you wait. . . relax. Enjoy your present state, and know that you are infinitely loved by your Creator, that He will deliver what He has promised, and that He cannot do otherwise because His divine, loving Intent is constant and unchangeable.

Meditate and prepare for sublime, divinely inspired joy to overwhelm and permeate your whole being very, very soon.

Θ   Θ   Θ

116   Many are experiencing pain and problems in their personal lives

The life changes and disruptions that many on Earth are experiencing at present are unsettling but unavoidable as all prepare for the move into full consciousness and full awareness of what it means to be human.

An understanding of why they are on Earth at this time is beginning to dawn on many, giving them a distinct sense that a new age is truly arriving, and that each one of them has a very important part to play. It is inspiring and exciting as well as unsettling, especially as so many are experiencing pain and problems in their personal lives and in their intimate relationships. Many unresolved issues from past lives, as well as from their present one, need to be addressed and released.

It is mainly a question of honestly accepting who you are, warts and all, and who your partners are, and then forgiving each other and allowing yourselves to be yourselves, instead of trying to create an unrealistic image of yourself to please close friends, authority figures, and cultural and religious institutions. Those "shoulds" and "not-good-enoughs" need to be released, so that you may relax into being you – the divinely created and infinitely loved entity that you truly are – for your own delight, and for the delight of all with whom you interact in any way at all.

That is your path, your destiny, your creative imperative. You chose to experience earth life to discover who you are, and to delight in that knowledge. You can do it right now! Just relax. . . listen to your heart, to your inner guidance, and know who you are. Your joy will be wondrous, as you finally recognize your Self. So do it — now.

Ө Ө Ө

117 When you move into your fully-conscious state. . .

We – all divinely created, fully-conscious entities – are on a continuous voyage of learning and discovery, as the divine One creates an ever-expanding range of activities for us to experience. The more there are, the more energy and motivation we have to learn and grow, unlike humanity which experiences overwhelm, overload, and then shuts down or goes into a small repetitive cycle of banal activities.

Soon, when you join us as fully-conscious beings, you too will find yourselves enjoying enthusiastic and boundless energy, enabling you to appreciate and participate wholeheartedly in your own new journeys of exploration and discovery. Never again will you be too bored, too tired, or just not interested enough to take advantage of the vast array of opportunities available to you. Each step you take in a process will be totally satisfying in itself. There will be absolutely no sense of having to complete a project or get a job done, because you will find that every moment of your existence is complete and satisfying.

It will be rather like walking through a beautifully planned and well-kept garden, where you see and smell the most lovely blossoms wherever you cast your glance, and each corner you turn brings some new enchantment. Yet, you can always retrace your steps to look again at something you have already seen and enjoyed. Whichever way you wander through this garden does not matter, for everywhere there will be sights and smells, views and sensations that will delight you.

And so it will be when you enter into full consciousness. In every moment you will enjoy the wonder of being alive, being aware, loving and being loved, respecting and being respected, because you are an essential, beautiful, irreplaceable, wholly conscious and wholly free part of God's divine creation. Without even one of you it would be incomplete. And yet the paradox is that creation is always complete in the sense (which is practically impossible to get a handle on) that all that is going to be, already is; and that all that is going to happen has already happened, and that all will continue to be and to happen.

When you move into your fully-conscious state, it will make absolute sense, and you will understand fully whatever you choose to understand. The possibilities and opportunities are boundless. And so will be your joy and exuberance in playing and working with them in the magnificent divine playground that the Creator has so delighted in preparing for you.

Ɵ   Ɵ   Ɵ

118   The divine plan can neither be derailed nor diverted

The world situation as presented by the mass media is always a very distorted image, as you well know. Continue to pray for change, for a fast resolution to humanity's problems worldwide, and know that it is already well underway behind the scenes.

Major healing is taking place planetwide as people increasingly seek purpose and meaning in their lives, leading them to greater levels of acceptance of and cooperation with others. And this is causing a tremendous shift in attitudes across the world. The mainstream media neither sees this nor wishes to see it, so it will not be reported. But all who are praying and intending for it know deep within themselves that it is truly happening.

The divine plan can neither be derailed nor diverted, and all who are attempting to cause disruptions to it are increasingly finding themselves confused and alarmed as their own plans and strategies come to nothing. The divine plan is flowing beautifully and smoothly, and the present stage is rapidly coming to a close.

No one's prayers or meditational energies have been wasted. Every intent and prayer for the Creator's plan to be divinely completed are being used most effectively. It could not be otherwise because the intentions of the millions of awakening souls on Planet Earth at this time provide an energy stream that is taken up by the divine realms and greatly intensified and strengthened.

Truly a moment of stupendous divine power and wonder is approaching very swiftly, heralding the arrival of the era to which you have all been looking forward, and which you have been most fervently intending to bring about. With the divine intensification and magnification of your own desires and intents to infinite proportions, no other outcome is even remotely possible.

As you know, deep within yourselves, all are rolling rapidly towards the Creator's divinely intended planetary awakening, so that an abundance of joy, delight, harmony, and wonder will very soon be yours, always, without end.

Θ Θ Θ

119 It is very difficult indeed for you to understand what is about to occur

As I have been telling you for some time, this stage in the Creator's divine plan for His creation is drawing to a close, and now, very rapidly indeed. I cannot stress enough how much we in the spiritual realms are looking forward to this magnificent, divine event, when all the lights ("lights" is, I'm afraid, a rather small and insignificant word to use to attempt to describe what I am talking about!) suddenly and instantaneously ignite in a blaze of divine and glorious brilliance that will bring you immediately home into full-conscious awareness of who you are and of your divine heritage.

Your delight and your joy will be stunning. And our joy in sharing your experience will be most wonderful.

The time for this stupendous and magnificent celebration of God's creation is truly almost upon us, and we will all be taking part in this sublimely exciting event – every divinely created, conscious entity. . . and there are so many of us! What a glorious party we are about to have.

I know it is very difficult for you, as humans, to understand or even imagine what is about to occur. And that will make it all the more wonderful for you when it does.

Continue to pray, relax, and meditate in preparation, and you will begin to open your awareness to let in, as it were, sneak previews of what to expect. They will be rather dim and blurry because that is all that you can experience without physical damage to your bodies. But hold the vision, and the new reality will arrive to delight you, and when that happens, your physical bodies will be ready to sail effortlessly into the new, divine environment that has been prepared for you.

Θ   Θ   Θ

120   Planetwide celebration will break out

Your earthly environment is changing very rapidly as the divine energies pour down from the heavenly realms to assist in the planet's cleansing and renewal. And these energies are having a very marked effect on humanity.

All of you have been seeking, praying, and hoping for a beautiful, peaceful, harmonious environment in which you can all live in peace and happiness, with all your needs and desires provided for abundantly. The divine One always hears and responds to your prayers – as you all know at the core of your being. And as the hopes and desires of humanity have come more and more into alignment, He has responded more and more powerfully to assist you to bring those desires to fruition.

You have free will, and in order for peace, joy, and harmony to exist on Earth, the great majority of humans must want it and intend that it come about. Over the last few decades, your desire for this state of being has intensified enormously. To use an analogy: light, as you generally experience it, is random and scattered, but you can see perfectly well with it to live your lives, whereas light from a laser is coherent and very finely focused; it enables many things to be achieved that are impossible with ordinary light.

So humanity's desire for peace, joy, and abundance has been like light that has become, particularly over the last few decades, more and more focused, and is now reaching a laser-like intensity, as all of you seek and desire Heaven on Earth.

This desire has now reached a keenness of focus which is so precise that the Will of the Creator and the will of humanity are coming into perfect alignment. The last few adjustments are now being made to perfect that alignment and will be completed very shortly, enabling this stage of the divine plan to reach completion and usher in – in one rapid and awesome moment – the new Golden Age of peace and abundance for which you have all been longing and praying for so long.

It truly is almost upon you now, and in a very short time planetwide joy, jubilation, and celebration will break out as the new age begins, and the old one – which was essential and perfect in its own way – simply fades away like an inconsequential dream.

Your prayers and meditations, your longing and your dreams are about to be fulfilled in a manner that at present is way beyond your wildest visions. Prepare to be amazed, awestruck, and overjoyed. You are on the home straight, and the finishing-line is clearly in sight, brilliantly lit, and you can hear the cheering of the enormous crowds waiting to welcome you home. And it truly will be a photo-finish as you all arrive together to celebrate, abundantly and magnificently, your marvelous achievement in bringing this stage of the divine plan to its most wonderful conclusion.

Your joy and ours will be immeasurable.

With so very much love from all of us in the spiritual realms as we await your arrival with the most eager anticipation.

Ɵ   Ɵ   Ɵ

121   Life is intended to be an absolute blast

Life is intended to be an absolute blast, and very soon now that is what it will become. Your Creator loves you all – utterly – completely – infinitely. And He wants you to have fun, to be happy, to be inspired and uplifted, so that you too can partake in the ever-ongoing and expanding divine creation which makes everything you can imagine possible.

The decision each one of you made to become human and to experience the troubles, pains, fears, and anxieties of your present environment was indeed inspired and heroic. It has been, as you are well aware, exceedingly demanding. But when you move into your fully-conscious state – as very soon you will – the reasons for your choice will become completely clear, and you will appreciate what marvels you have achieved and realize that that has always been your intention.

Your coming delight and satisfaction – rewards, if you like, for what you have achieved – have been well earned, and that you will also understand. So continue firmly and intently on your path while focusing on the fact that you have almost reached its end. You will find that you truly have the energy, the desire, and the enthusiasm to do your part in bringing this stage of the divine plan to its most wonderful, divinely ordained conclusion, for the delight and joy of the Creator and all His creation, which of course includes each of you!

Ө   Ө   Ө

122   The Creator will announce the instantaneous start of the new Golden Age

Much is happening in the spiritual realms as the final preparations for this monumental event advance rapidly towards conclusion. There is a tremendous energy exchange in progress at present between Heaven and Earth. And those of you who know of the coming Golden Age, and are on Earth to prepare for it and welcome its arrival, are doing much work in the spiritual realms, much more than you are accustomed to, which is very tiring indeed for your physical bodies. Take what rest you need; avoid strong physical effort, as your energy is required and being used on higher levels. . . and otherwise relax. Stop the endless chattering of your minds, and focus on living in the present moment.

The final preparations are very nearly over, and the last check on the state of readiness of all involved – and there are very many – will soon take place. Once that is done the divine Creator will announce, at precisely the appropriate moment, the end of the present age and the instantaneous start of the new Golden Age for which all have been waiting.

In the spiritual realms the excited anticipation is quite palpable. We wait, as it were, with bated breath as the countdown approaches its end. All who are consciously aware of the divine program, and their place in it, can feel the tension and excitement mount, because soon all disharmony, disease, dissatisfaction, misunderstanding, hostility, anger, and desire for vengeance will dissolve, as all become aware of what they have really been doing and what they have achieved.

Harmony, delight, wonder, joy, and love will inundate Planet Earth as never before, infecting all instantaneously. It will truly be as though you had been asleep and dreaming, and then awoke to find yourselves at the most magnificent celebratory party, where all your wishes had been granted and all your dreams had come true. You will want for nothing, and what you have will provide you with boundless satisfaction and contentment that is also uplifting and exhilarating.

The Creator's Love for all of you knows no bounds, and His delight in your joy will be most wonderful to experience and to behold. This stage of the divine endeavor has taken eons to approach completion, because it is so magnificent in concept and in execution.

There is no conscious being within the divine creation who will not be utterly amazed and delighted beyond all imaginative powers when the great moment dawns. It is difficult to describe how close it is, especially for you on Earth who have only a faint sense of this wholly magnificent event that will suddenly change your lives totally, completely, and forever.

The magnificence of this event will be spell-binding, enthralling, exciting far beyond your present ability to be excited. Deep within each one of you, you know this – you have always known it. And yet it appears to be almost completely hidden from you.

Part of your great delight when the moment comes, will be the instantaneous recognition that this is what you have been working towards for all these eons of time, and that it is what you have achieved by your intense efforts, powerfully aided by the Creator and all in the divine realms.

It has been a momentous and marvelous cooperative venture, in which all have played their parts with great competence and professionalism in bringing the multitudes of strands together at this precise moment of completion. The great event will be miraculous, overwhelming all with the power of the Divine.

Prepare to enjoy yourselves enormously – and soon!

⊖   ⊖   ⊖

123   Divine promises are never broken

Growing as a human from infancy to adulthood is a very difficult and demanding experience. The pressures from family, school, social and religious groups, demanding that you conform to an agreed form of behavior, way of thinking, and way of perceiving the environmental reality that you inhabit, are very strong.

Yet each entity who chooses existence as a human has decided to develop its own individual and unique qualities. Even so, most entities incarnate into environments where the true meaning of freedom and individual rights is either unknown, or understood in only the most limited fashion. Consequently, enormous amounts of energy are needed just for survival.

Survival frequently becomes the entity's overriding concern, and the plan it had created for itself prior to incarnation becomes buried under a vast accumulation of ethnic, cultural, and religious or atheistic sludge. To recognize this and to delve into it to recover its plan is not easy, which is why so many humans are lost and confused and believe life to be a once-only experience with no "before" or "after." And that is an extremely depressing prospect because the entity cannot help but become aware that that perception really makes no sense at all.

Of course each entity experiencing human existence has deep within itself the certain knowledge that it is a part of All That Is, that it exists eternally, and that it is constantly bathed in the Creator's Light, and enveloped in His Love.

However, having chosen to experience life as a human, it accepted the conditions, or rules of the game, that being human entails. For most entities this means that during infancy and early childhood, as physical strength grows with increasing bodily size and a sense of familiarity with its environment develops, its faint memories of its spiritual heritage – essential for initial survival during and immediately after birth – slowly fade. This allows the child to develop its humanity, complete with all the conditioning that the total environment in which it has chosen to experience life imposes on it.

In late adolescence or early adulthood, as the human that the entity has become develops a sense of adult independence – to a greater or lesser degree – the very faint memories of its spiritual heritage return to encourage it to become aware of the fact that there is far more to life as a human than it had supposed. Once its curiosity has been aroused in this way, it has the ability to go within and begin to discover for itself the wonders available to it as part of God's divine and infinitely loving creation.

Of course, frequently, earthly distractions succeed in holding the entity's attention and in engaging it constantly on the physical, mental, and emotional levels of human existence. From time to time, a sense of longing or dissatisfaction will creep into its awareness, or these may crop up suddenly and very noticeably. And this of course is a wake-up call from the higher or spiritual Self. And again, often this call is brushed aside and ignored.

When the reality of human death comes firmly into awareness – as it always will – it can often cause fear and confusion and the sense that the entity has missed out on something most important (which it has), leading to a closing down of the awareness in order to relieve the pain and anguish that the sense of having wasted its life causes.

And there are entities who maintain a hold on their spiritual memories throughout their whole lives, and who never get lost or totally wrapped up in the environmental distractions by which they are surrounded. These entities provide wake-up calls on the physical level to those who have become lost and confused. This makes it easier for the lost ones, as they relate to these more spiritually developed humans, to become aware that there is far more to life than they had imagined.

So it is apparent that to incarnate as a human is a very difficult and demanding task, but the rewards it brings far outweigh the disadvantages.

As a human you cannot fail – that is impossible! God promised you that He would always be there for you, wherever you are and whatever you do. Divine promises are never broken – they absolutely cannot be.

So, whatever you experience during your human existence – from the deepest depths of pain, anguish, and despair, to the highest form of joy and ecstasy that you can imagine – it can only lead you back to the infinite bliss that has always been promised to you. That is your birthright, and it is the reason that you were created.

You are, always have been, and always will be, infinitely loved by God. And you are infinitely worthy of that divine Love.

Trust yourself. . . your true Self. . . not the socially conditioned self that you usually present to the world. Honor and respect yourself and others, as God does, and know and experience His Love for you and for all His creation, of which, as you have always known, you are an absolutely essential part.

Θ   Θ   Θ

124   Every human is involved

Change is in the air very palpably, and very many people are feeling it.

Your planet is being absolutely inundated with the most powerful energies from the divine realms, and these are being welcomed, customized, and distributed planetwide as necessary and appropriate by the millions upon millions of you who pray and meditate regularly.

Every single human in prayer or meditation, desiring change in attitudes and perceptions by humanity, to permit and encourage love, spiritual growth, awareness, and harmony to develop and blossom on Planet Earth, truly has an enormous effect. Any of you who feel that your prayer or meditation is of little use, please look around you and observe the wonderful changes that are occurring. See the compassion, the concern, and the love that so many are expressing by their way of living. You must look and see it for yourselves wherever you happen to be. . . kind words and friendly looks in the most unexpected places.

This is a vast intent for change that is rapidly gaining momentum.

The unmitigated bad news from the mainstream media about violence, prejudice, and conflict all over your planet are in fact the last remnants of the energy of fear – distrust, suspicion, judgment, bigotry – that have been pervasive for eons on Planet

Earth, and which are now dissolving in the flood of divine Love that is enveloping Earth.

As more and more of you awaken to your inbuilt need and desire to love and be loved, and make that intent a part of every moment of your existence, you truly bring it about.

Concentrate on seeing the divine spark in everyone you interact with in any way whatever, from deep intimate personal relationships, to people you just brush past in a crowd, and respond with love in every situation, even when you feel threatened or under attack.

Just send out love to embrace the other(s) and see the tension in a situation ease, and even dissolve altogether. Remember that by changing yourself you change the world.

Living with love constantly in your hearts for absolutely everyone, no matter how obnoxious they may appear to be, has a miraculous effect; people around you no longer feel a need to be alert and ready to go on the offensive in response to an attack. They relax, communication occurs, and problems and difficulties are resolved almost effortlessly.

The more open and accepting you can be, the more you will experience love. Love will surround you, and your personal environment will become increasingly harmonious. And as more and more people do likewise, these areas of harmony will start to connect and interact with each other. The individual pools of harmony will interlink to form ponds, lakes, seas, and finally great oceans. It is happening right now, all around you.

So join in and truly discover your life purpose.

Every human is involved; it is just that many have not yet realized it. But each one who awakens affects all in his vicinity, and so others awaken, and the harmony and loving intelligence spreads, leading to planetwide healing and renewal.

All are infinitely, divinely loved – they always have been and always will be – and they are beginning to awaken and become aware of it. Spring is truly in the air as new growth breaks out everywhere. Look around you and see it. . . and participate in this divine renewal, and delight in it as only you can.

Yes, each one of you will experience it in your own individual and unique way, while also being conscious of your Oneness with all others and with your heavenly Father.

Ɵ Ɵ Ɵ

125   An entity choosing to be human is greatly honored in other realms

The human life experience that an entity undergoes in its intentional search for spiritual growth and wisdom is indeed a wonderful thing.

In its non-physical state, an entity has available to it an infinite source of knowledge, wisdom, and information, and an infinite selection of choices through which to experience itself. Choosing a human experience is a remarkable choice, because the entity knows that by so doing it will enter a realm in which it seems that its prior existence had never happened. It will "forget" all that it had ever known or learnt, and will start over – apparently from scratch – to try and learn about and understand the purpose (if any!) of existence. (The entity may at times even wonder if it really exists at all!)

Frequently, it chooses a path that, in human terms, causes it much pain, anger, doubt, and confusion, with a continuous underlying sense of abandonment and worthlessness. These feelings and experiences provide the equivalent of a very rich and fertile soil in which its seed of spirituality can grow strong

226

and flourish. But in doing so, it does have to contend with the various parasites and diseases that feed on healthy growth. Always it has all it needs to withstand these apparently virulent attacks, and yet frequently it seems to succumb, falling into anger, hate, and fear, and so needing once again to experience life as a human.

Once an entity makes the choice to be human, it has to stay with that choice until it has fully worked its way through it to total acceptance and unconditional love of itself. This is why an entity choosing to be human is so honored, loved, and respected in other realms, where the difficulty of the task undertaken is so clearly understood.

When the entity chooses to become human, it absolutely knows that it will succeed in completely fulfilling the tasks that it has set itself, and that it will eventually overcome its apparent feelings of abandonment and worthlessness, to return to its infinitely joyful and blissful Unity with the Divine.

Before it embarks on the journey, it has an understanding of the difficulties of the tasks involved, and has the most glorious vision of what it will be like when they are all satisfactorily completed. What it does not know is how many incarnations it will take to complete its journey, but it is quite happy about this lack of knowledge because it knows of the magnificent rewards it will receive on completion, and because that completion is guaranteed by the divine Being.

Setting out on this journey, this path of human existence, the entity is surrounded by the light of the most magnificent brilliance from all the guides who will continuously follow it on its path, monitoring its progress, and feeding it in abundance the energies that it needs at any given moment to ensure its success. The entity is never alone – let alone abandoned! – even though it may seem to experience this very condition painfully and repeatedly. If it was truly alone and abandoned, it would just cease to exist. Never forget that.

The fact that you exist proves beyond any possibility of doubt that you are totally loved by your Creator, and that you are always accompanied by the guides most suited to assist you at any particular moment of your human life. You are always utterly loved, and absolutely never alone.

So meditate – open your hearts and allow your guides to enter and fill you with the love that is your divine right from your loving Creator.

Ɵ   Ɵ   Ɵ

126   Eventually, all will take part, all will be one

As you grow and develop spiritually, your life will feel far more satisfying and balanced. In the early stages of growth, just like a young plant, you are vulnerable to all kinds of minor disturbances which can slow down or actually halt your growth. However, as you develop and grow, your resilience increases, and it takes a much larger or stronger disturbance to unsettle you.

There will always be disturbances, because coping with them is an essential part of each individual's life path. It is important to realize and to be constantly aware that you will never experience an upset or disturbance that you are unable to surmount. Everything that occurs in your life has been especially tailored to provide you with learning-opportunities that are in every way appropriate for the stage of your life in which they occur.

The life plan that each one of you lives is extremely elegant and practical. It matters not whether you overcome each difficulty as it arises – or keep failing to do so – because your life plan is infinitely flexible, and will always provide you with the experience you need in that moment. Whether you use each experience to the fullest, or continually choose not to, the next moment will always provide you with exactly what you need to move on, and with as much help as you choose to accept.

The Creator's plan for each individual provides an elegant and totally appropriate life path that supplies abundantly – but never wastefully – precisely what each of you truly needs in every moment, because each one of you was very much involved in its planning.

Just accept and allow, and it will flow through you constantly and miraculously at precisely the flow rate that is in perfect harmony and synchronicity with the frequencies of your own perfect energies. A most beautiful blending of spiritual forces will create harmony within you, inviting you to dance, sing, and laugh your way through life. This is the way your heavenly Father created you. And doing this brings you back to a state of Oneness, of Unity, of connection and integration with Him.

And when you move into this state of Oneness – and all will move into it – your awareness of your individuality will be most wonderfully increased and expanded. It is a divine paradox of the most beautiful, amazing, and exhilarating intensity that can be neither described or imagined – it can only be experienced.

Open yourselves. Accept and experience this divine wonder. It is God's intention that you should. Creation is being. Creation is ever ongoing. And you are part of creation, as creation is part of you. Nothing and no one is left out or excluded, because then creation would be incomplete. And that is not possible. . . because creation is All That Is.

Wake up. Pull away from your myopic focus on the anxieties of daily living. Don't go back to sleep. Open yourselves completely – now – to His Love, and be what He and you have always intended: an ongoing unlimited experience of love, peace, and harmony, in continuously increasing intensity.

Creation is a song, a divine and harmonious expression of brilliance and beauty, in which all are invited to take part. Each one who joins in this divine song of creation supplies an individual vibration of great intensity that adds immeasurably to the richness of the whole, without which it cannot be complete and which cannot be provided in any other way.

Eventually all will take part, all will be One. So why delay? There is nothing particularly advantageous or beneficial about delayed gratification! Open your hearts now, not tomorrow, or next year, or next lifetime. There is absolutely no need to delay until you are "without sin," "perfect," "absolved," "forgiven." That has already happened! Enjoy now. Enjoy all that you are, and by so doing, you assist others to do the same.

ϴ ϴ ϴ

127 You are beginning to sense that great changes of enormous significance are on the verge of happening

Humanity – the inhabitants of Planet Earth – is about to move into the new divine and Golden Age that has been promised for so long. Many preparations and arrangements were necessary to enable this to come about, and they have been in progress for a very long time, as humanity experiences it. Now those eons of preparation and planning have come to an end, and it is time for the new, divine era

This is hard for you on Earth to imagine or foresee, because you have been experiencing quite a different kind of existence for a very long time, and your awareness of your various earthly histories continues to remind you of the unsatisfactory nature of life on Earth.

Your remembrance of your experience in the spiritual or heavenly realms has been hidden from you during your lives as humans, and you have had only yearnings and intimations that existence could and should be far, far better than anything you have experienced. Those yearnings have been the rocks, the firm foundations on which you have built your hopes and prayers and from which you have directed them to God.

This tough human existence which you have been experiencing – and even those who seem to have everything it is materially possible to have are having a tough time – is to all intents and purposes over. There are just a few minor details to be cleared up before your prayers for divine deliverance from the daily grind of earthly existence are answered most magnificently.

Your experience as humans on Earth has been a very hard struggle for the great majority of you – a struggle that you undertook in the full knowledge that it would produce rewards and delights of unimaginable magnificence once it was completed.

Completion is about to occur, and when it does you will find yourselves living in the environment of untold beauty and exuberance of which you have been dreaming for so long. You are going to move into a world of the utmost peace and harmony. It is a state that it is impossible for us in the spiritual realms to describe for you, or for you in your present state of very limited perceptual abilities to imagine.

However, within every one of you now, your inner God-given knowing deep in your hearts is beginning to awaken, to come out of its long period of slumber. You are beginning to sense that great changes of enormous significance are on the verge of happening.

And, Dear Ones, you are absolutely correct. The Creator's divine environment of utmost joy and happiness is about to envelop you totally, completely, and forever. So continue to pray, meditate, or just relax, knowing – truly knowing, as you do in the depths of your being – that your release from this tough and demanding environment into His divine realm of infinite perfection is almost upon you.

Much of humanity has been so sunk in the depths of what could be described as a pea-soup fog, an extremely long night, or indeed a coma, that your sudden and magical awakening will be absolutely stunning for you. It will be a shock of unimaginable proportions, followed immediately by the most wondrous sense of unbridled joy and happiness, as you realize that you have arrived Home, and find yourselves surrounded and lifted on high by throngs of your most dearly loved relatives and friends, whom it seems you have not seen, or even remembered, for a very long time. The joy and wonder that you are all about to experience, very soon now, will be absolutely magnificent.

Ɵ   Ɵ   Ɵ

128   You have carried dreams of paradise deep within you for so very long

Much is going on as the preparations for humanity's move into full consciousness approach completion. You have all waited for this very patiently for a long time, and you will most certainly not be disappointed.

A event of unprecedented importance is about to occur, which will bring great joy to billions of humans across Planet Earth. It

232

will be an event of amazing significance for humanity and the planet because it will completely change the way you live and the way you experience life itself. It will be Heaven on Earth, Shambhala, and all will be overjoyed and inspired to be creative in ways they have never before imagined. Your way of life will be divinely inspired in every moment and you will want for nothing, as everything you could ever desire will be instantly available.

This does not mean luxury cars or homes, or the most wonderful lovers, because when you become fully conscious and become aware of what is possible, your desires and wishes will be far beyond anything you can presently imagine. Moreover, you will no longer need to work or save up for them. Your material wants and desires in the world are very ephemeral, and when you move into full consciousness their appeal to you will truly pale into insignificance when you realize who you are, where you are, and what is available to you.

It is impossible to give you even the smallest idea of what has been prepared for you, but it will be way beyond extreme, lifting you to levels of happiness and satisfaction of which you could never even conceive.

As this marvelous moment approaches, rapidly now, our delight here in the spiritual realms is growing in intensity because we can understand how great your joy is going to be. We eagerly await the fulfillment of the dreams of paradise that you have carried deep within you for so very long.

The party is about to commence, as the preparations are almost complete. So prepare yourselves for total joy – it is about to envelop you!

Ɵ   Ɵ   Ɵ

129   Harmonious energy-melding is the most powerful force in the universe

As life rushes busily along in your three-dimensional environment, it is extremely easy to get caught up in, captivated by, and totally distracted from your life's true purpose by the frenetic activity you see and experience all around you.

One of life's many purposes is to show you the two extremes – frenetic activity and total passivity – so that you may establish your own place, your personal, balanced state between the two. The physical point between these extremes – where their charismatic attractions hold you comfortably balanced, pulling you neither one way nor the other, but allowing you to swing gently, a little way back and forth as in a hammock – depend on your body chemistry, your cultural and genetic inheritance, and your chosen life path.

The point of balance, the comfort zone, is different for everyone. And it is important that each individual find his own place, and that parents encourage their children to find theirs, instead of trying to define it for them.

For human relationships of any sort to be harmonious, it is essential that each individual be securely established in their own comfort zone, and to accept that others belong in their own comfort zones. This enables relationships to expand creatively. Attempting to persuade or manipulate another into accepting your comfort zone as the right place for them causes unnecessary tension and friction. This leads to judgment, which drives the joint creative energy patterns between the individuals to distort and then interfere with each other, leading to conflict or stagnation instead of allowing them to flow harmoniously and synergistically together in a marvelous melding of energies as the Creator intends.

Harmonious energy-melding is the most powerful creative force in the universe, and to succeed in bringing it to fruition on Earth and throughout the Milky Way Galaxy is one of the main reasons for humanity's presence on the planet at this time. The melding or fusion of powerful energies to enhance and continue the divine creative plan was set in motion before time existed.

Love is the great energy. It can combine all other separated energies into one massive flowing ocean of divine Intent, synergistically and harmoniously expanding infinitely and forever. It cannot be stopped.

However, it can be diverted. Energies of hate, separation, and conflict are like low dry mounds on relatively flat ground that has been flooded. As the flood waters (Love) rise, the mounds disappear; the water becomes one, covering and smoothing into itself these arid areas of disharmony.

Humanity's growth into loving awareness of its unity with the Creator – the task on which you are all now working so energetically and successfully – is approaching completion, as the abundant divine energies pour down on the planet in an all-encompassing, soothing flood that is rapidly deepening to the point at which it will no longer be possible to divert it.

Those who would divert these energies will be swept away to where they can continue their development without hindering or delaying those who are ready to realize, recognize, and return to their divine blissful state of harmonious union with the divine Dynamic.

Ө   Ө   Ө

130 Your awareness and all mental abilities will expand enormously

Life flows energetically all the time, sweeping along with it the flotsam and jetsam, the waste and the trash, all that lies in its path. Nothing gets left behind as it carries all before it, clearing and cleansing the path that it is creating in preparation for environmental changes of great importance for the well-being of Planet Earth.

The Earth is undergoing a transformation which will enrich and enliven it and all the life forms it supports, as it moves into the true New Age for which all – knowingly or unknowingly – have been waiting and preparing.

This new Golden Age will be a time of enlightenment for all who are ready; and all those who wish it and intend it are ready!

Spiritual development has always been possible and accessible to humanity. And now humanity is seeking it on a scale and with an intensity of purpose not seen here before. The divine Creator honors that intent and increases the empowering energies flowing to the planet and its life forms. This leads to increasing awareness which further intensifies the planet's spiritual desire and intent, allowing the Creator to further enhance the empowering energies. A movement of great strength is then established with an ever-increasing momentum, drawing all upwards towards the spiritual heritage that is their birthright.

This dawning awareness affects all, leading them forward in hope – a hope that until recently very few had experienced – generating an energy of cooperation and harmony which allows much to be accomplished that would previously have been believed impossible, due to the distrustful and competitive nature of human relations.

Very soon you will move into full consciousness, and your awareness and all your mental abilities will expand enormously, giving you the power you need to understand and operate in the dawning Golden Age that is almost upon you.

This path was planned a very long time ago, and you are very nearly ready to join it and move rapidly ahead in order to start fulfilling the contract that all your preparations have been leading up to.

The apparent lack of purpose that many of you have felt in your lives has been a protective cover or shield you chose to install so that you would not be distracted from your preparations, which have been moving along very well indeed. I know that you find it hard to believe that you have been preparing in any way at all, but that is because your shield has hidden from your present consciousness anything that would distract you from those preparations, which at your level of awareness seem to be non-existent.

In fact, you have been doing an incredible amount of preparation that is now coming to fruition, and that will enable you so elegantly and competently to move consciously forward when the moment is right. At that time the shield will drop, all will fall into place, you will be amazed to see what you have achieved and to see the new path on which you are about to embark. Hang in there; all is proceeding as divinely intended towards your divine destiny.

Ө   Ө   Ө

Our Divine Destiny

About Saul and John.

I have been taking dictation from my friend Saul since 1995. Prior to that I had for some years been reading many channeled books, and had found them inspiring and uplifting. I wondered "Could I perhaps channel a loving spiritual entity?" Then one day in 1995 I sat down, pen in hand, and asked "Please may I make contact now with a guide of high spiritual development to help me with my spiritual growth and life purpose, and anything else that would be beneficial to God's Will for humanity?" I got an immediate response!

"Good evening John – welcome to channeling. Energy changes are necessary for good communications. Talking is difficult – light will intensify as our channel opens to communication. There is much to talk about and we will need much time. Energy for writing is provided to enable a smooth flow of information. ... Life is the greatest gift imaginable. It expresses intent to grow and create a kaleidoscope of experiences which lead to self-understanding that can only be dreamt of in other realms. . . You see it is easy to channel information, I will help you to establish clear communication with me, if you so wish."

And that is how I started channeling Saul. He is a spiritual entity whose messages over the years have inspired and uplifted me, and the time has come to share those messages. May they inspire all who read them.